Simple Accounting

May also be used as a Study Guide

By

Dantes Joseph Jr.

ISBN: 1-4033-6218-1 (e-book)
ISBN: 1-4033-6219-X (Paperback)

This book is printed on acid free paper.

1stBooks – rev. 12/27/02

Introduction

Financial accounting has always been a very interesting field of study. It has also been a challenging area because the material is not always easy to grasp the first time around. It is imperative that as you study accounting, you get a bigger and bigger picture of the whole accounting cycle. You are going to learn that accounting has to do with gathering, sorting, recording and posting financial information in order to produce the ultimate end product: **The Financial Statements**. Users of the financial statements include management in a company, government authorities, creditors and investors. The financial statements tell us the results of operations and the financial position of a company at a given point in time. Investors use <u>audited</u> financial statements in order to make decisions as to whether or not to invest their hard-earned money in a company.

You, as an accountant, therefore will play a very important role. You will either be involved with processing the raw data that is needed to prepare the financial information that will be used by the general public, or you will be one who will analyze the finished product in order to render an opinion as to the fairness of the information. These individuals are referred to as <u>Auditors</u>. An auditor is still an accountant, however he goes beyond preparing the financial information: he reviews them and decides whether or not they are produced in conformity with certain government regulations that we will talk about in this book. These auditors frequently bear the title of <u>Certified Public Accountant (CPA)</u>. You can be an accountant and not be an auditor. However, you cannot be an auditor without first having been an accountant.

As long as you can keep in the back of your mind that the ultimate objective of accounting is to produce financial information that will be used by the general public, you will be on the right track and the material will not be so difficult to understand. As you do this, you will also begin to have a global view of the entire accounting cycle in your mind so that you will know where you are every step of the way.

In this book we will look at a lot of the <u>basic concepts</u> of accounting. These are the groundwork of the whole accounting profession. You will need to get a solid understanding of these principles before you go to any intermediate or advance courses. This is where you will have the most fun. The material is not too difficult. I have taken steps to simplify these principles so that you not only learn, but also enjoy it.

Table of Contents

Chapter 1

Job Opportunities In Accounting

Do I need to be good at math to do well in accounting?

I'd like to share my personal experience with you. I went to Rockland Community College; a 2 year school in Rockland County NY. I was coming to the last semester, having taken a lot of general courses because I was not yet sure what I wanted to major in. I thought, like most people, I'd take Business Administration. I'm sure a lot of people don't really know what that major really is. It just seems to be a general field that should satisfy the demands they face to graduate college. Anyway, I had to take Financial Accounting in order to graduate. I took a look at the accounting textbook the other students were carrying around and I freaked out! Not only was the book a thick one, I saw a lot of numbers on the hard cover that seemed to indicate that there is a great deal of math involved. I know that math was not one of my strong points. I didn't know what I was going to do.

Since I needed to take the class to graduate, I did just that. The class was scheduled to meet at 9 a.m. on Saturday mornings. Our professor was a CPA (a Certified Payne in the you know what) just kidding! CPA stands for Certified Public Accountant. He used to walk with a limp because he had a bad leg. The class started off with about 35 students. I'll never forget the instructor being very up-front with the class in telling us that we had to concentrate very hard on the subject matter in order to pass his course. He went on to say that we could not have more than a certain number of absences, I don't remember how many; something like 3 or 4 for the entire semester. He argued that accounting is not like other classes. In other classes, if you miss one day, you can get notes from another student and catch up. Accounting however has a staircase effect on your overall learning: every subject is built upon the previous one. If you missed a

1

topic on "prepaid expense" for example, the next time it's discussed it will not be explained again. The teacher would move into other things like "amortization" or "posting to the general ledger."

The professor went on and on about how tough the course was and the fact that we should not expect to pass based on our good looks! Needless to say that the first week he lost about 5 to 8 students. Some just could not handle the pressure. Every week or every other week he would lose some more students. By the time we got to the final exam, we had only 5 students left in the class. Surprisingly enough I was one of them. It turned out that I did really well in the class. I realized that math is a very incidental thing in accounting. I've always said that the highest level of math that you will ever need in your entire accounting career is probably basic algebra. Everything else is pretty straightforward and includes your basic "addition, subtraction, multiplication and division". I know a lot of people are not really good with division and I am one of them. However, that should not stop you from being a good accountant. The more you work at it, the more comfortable you will become.

The key to success in accounting is #1 patience and #2 organization. I quickly began to understand why I liked the subject and got an "A" in the class. I am an organized person. I like things to be clean, well kept and logical. When I saw that accounting had to do with gathering raw data from various sources in order to prepare the ultimate end product: The Financial Statements; and to get to that point, <u>debits</u> have to equal <u>credits,</u> Believe it or not, I found that to be fun. I did so well in that class that the teacher was asking me if I would help him out in his office on a part-time basis. He also suggested that I continued in that field of study. This is exactly what happened. I went on to a 4-year school where I maintained my 4.0 average in accounting right through my advance courses. My overall GPA was around a 3.4.

This should be a general guide to all of you to see if accounting is the right field for you. If you find that you hate to balance your checkbook, you may think seriously about whether or not to become an accountant. If you find that balancing the checkbook is a challenge; and that you are not at ease until you've defeated that challenge and find a sense of satisfaction in doing it, then you should do very well in accounting.

What can I expect to do with my accounting skills?

There is a VAST demand for accountants in the world. I have seen small businesses start out with the goal of selling a product or a service. The owners get excited about having their own business and so they go and rent space to get their activities going. Later on they are faced with keeping track of income and expenses in order to apply for a loan. Banks will generally ask for financial statements to see just how well a business is doing before they will lend money to it. In addition small business owners are faced with high expenses like "rent" and because their business is new in the market place, their income has not yet come to the level they need to meet various obligations that they are faced with. They are also faced with the need to communicate with the federal and state government through income taxes and business regulations. Unless they plan ahead and anticipate these problems, they will be bogged down and it will become more and more difficult for them to continue to operate their business.

Many businesses therefore end up having to close down. The owners did not plan carefully before starting out. A lot of people start businesses out of their own home to keep costs down until they can begin to build a clientele. When they feel they have reached a certain comfort level, they will then go out and rent space to continue building their business. This, by the way is an excellent way to start a business provided that you can get an occupational license that will allow you to run a business from your home. This is getting very popular today and many businesses start out that way.

As an accountant you will be called upon to provide the following services:

- Accounting and bookkeeping
- Business planning and consulting
- Preparing payroll and payroll taxes
- Preparing the financial statements
- Auditing the financial statements
- Preparing company income taxes
- Preparing company property taxes etc.

There is a great demand for accountants and auditors. Think of it this way: every single business that exists needs an accountant. Many times also individuals for one reason or other will need accountants. They may want you to help them in preparing a Trust or a Will where there are a lot of assets involved. You may have to prepare Personal Financial Statements for them for a variety of reasons.

Every company will have to file income taxes with the government. They will need to file payroll as well as year-end income taxes. You are the accountant that will assist with these needs. It is no wonder; therefore that accounting has always been a high-demand field. My advice to all accounting students is to start by working in public accounting after graduation. You should become an auditor and work for a public accounting firm that provides services like auditing, bookkeeping and taxes. The reason for this is that you will quickly get an overall picture of the accounting cycle. You will be working with a variety of clients in different industries. This will give you a broader view of the different accounting needs and you will gain a great deal of experience that will allow you to work for yourself or as a Chief Financial Officer (CFO) for a major company once you decide to become stable.

Service vs. Merchandising

Once you are ready to work in the real world, you will need to decide which industry will work best for you. You may also develop a certain preference for working in service type businesses instead of a merchandising concern. Service companies are those who provide a service as opposed to buying merchandise to re-sell for a profit. The advantage of working in a service type industry is that you will not have to compute costs related to merchandise purchased nor will you have to worry about valuing the company's merchandise inventory.

No matter which area you choose to work in, there is a tremendous amount of opportunity in both. Accountants and auditors have always been and always will be in high demand, as advancement in technology tends to create more and more businesses. Even with the advent of computer software that significantly reduces the time spent in recording and posting accounting data, this does not eliminate the need for accountants. The accountant is still needed to interpret, analyze and report on financial information crucial to various companies.

4

Chapter 2

Lawmakers

Accounting, like any other profession, is regulated by various regulatory bodies. Regulation is good because it helps to establish trust and credibility in the profession and in those who practice it, namely the Certified Public Accountants (CPAs). Remember the CPA is licensed to practice accounting on the public level; that is he or she is capable of signing audit reports on financial statements that will be used by the general public.

Generally Accepted Accounting Principles (GAAP)

This is a set of uniform accounting rules, standards and procedures for recording and reporting financial data to accurately represent an organization's financial condition. It was created by the Financial Accounting Standards Board (FASB) and the Securities and Exchange Commission (SEC) requires their use for corporations under its jurisdiction.

The Financial Accounting Standards Board (FASB)

The mission of the Financial Accounting Standards Board is to establish and improve standards of financial accounting and reporting for the guidance and education of the public, including issuers, auditors, and users of financial information.

Since 1973, the FASB has been the designated organization in the private sector for establishing standards of financial accounting and reporting. Those standards govern the preparation of financial reports. They are officially recognized as authoritative by the Securities and Exchange Commission and the American Institute of Certified Public Accountants. Such standards are essential to the efficient functioning of the economy because investors, creditors, auditors and others rely on credible, transparent and comparable financial information. The FASB was previously known as the Accounting Principles Board (APB) from 1959 to 1973.

The American Institute of Certified Public Accountants (AICPA)

The American Institute of Certified Public Accountants and its predecessors have a history dating back to 1887, when the American Association of Public Accountants was formed. In 1916, the American Association was succeeded by the Institute of Public Accountants, at which time there was a membership of 1,150. The name was changed to the American Institute of Accountants in 1917 and remained so until 1957, when the name was again changed to the American Institute of Certified Public Accountants. The American Society of Certified Public Accountants was formed in 1921 and acted as a federation of state societies. The Society was merged into the Institute in 1936 and, at that time, the Institute agreed to restrict its future members to CPAs.

The AICPA is the national, professional organization for all Certified Public Accountants (CPAs). Its mission is to provide members with the resources, information, and leadership that enable them to provide valuable services in the highest professional manner to benefit the public as well as employers and clients. In fulfilling its mission, the AICPA works with state CPA organizations and gives priority to those areas where public reliance on CPA skills is most significant.

The Securities and Exchange Commission (SEC)

The Securities and Exchange Commission (SEC) has statutory authority to establish financial accounting and reporting standards for publicly held companies under the Securities Exchange Act of 1934. Throughout its history, however, the Commission's policy has been to rely on the private sector for this function to the extent that the private sector demonstrates ability to fulfill the responsibility in the public interest.

The Internal Revenue Service (IRS)

The Internal Revenue Service (IRS) is the nation's tax collection agency and administers the Internal Revenue Code enacted by Congress. Its mission is to provide America's taxpayers with top quality service by helping them understand and meet their tax responsibilities and by applying the tax law with integrity and fairness to all.

The IRS plays a very important role in the accounting profession. You will learn the various methods of calculating book depreciation in the lessons to come. However the IRS establishes its own accelerated method of depreciation called Accelerated Cost Recovery System (ACRS). You will learn about accelerated depreciation methods acceptable under GAAP. However, we will not discuss at this time the difference between the two. In both cases it is a way of accelerating depreciation on an asset in order to recover its cost more quickly. ACRS as defined by the Internal Revenue Code (tax law) is discussed in tax related courses.

The accountant will be intimately involved with the IRS in preparing a variety of tax returns for a company. Both on the payroll level as well as year-end tax returns for the company itself.

Chapter 3

Fundamental Accounting Principles

Business Organizations

There are generally three types of business organizations:

        a- Proprietorship
        b- Partnerships
        c- Corporations

Proprietorship

A proprietorship is one that is owned and operated by a single individual. If John decides to open up a coffee shop by himself and call it John's Coffee Shop, he becomes the proprietor of that business. He is his own boss. He establishes the rules and regulations that will govern his business. He will work hard to try and please his customers in order for him to stay in business. The advantages of such an organization is that it is very easy to form. He would simply file under the <u>fictitious names act</u> in the state in which he operates and then he's in business. The disadvantage for him owning a business under his name like this is that he has <u>unlimited liability.</u> This means that he is personally liable for all debts and obligations of his company. If he ever got sued for a large sum of money and the business was not enough to satisfy the suite, the law may even take away personal property that he owns like a house, car or jewelry to satisfy the judgment.

When he files his income tax return at the end of the year, he will report the income and expenses of his coffee shop on a separate form

8

and include it together with his own taxes to determine how much tax he is liable for.

Partnerships

A partnership is where two or more people get together to accomplish a business transaction or to organize a business, which would have otherwise been too large for a single individual. Bob and Mary may bring their knowledge and expertise together in order to form a business. Bob maybe good at cutting hair; Mary maybe good at doing manicures and pedicures. So they decide to open a salon together and call it "The Beauty Salon, unlimited". The advantages again have to do with the fact that it's easy to operate. They will share responsibilities among themselves and recording the business will require that they file under the fictitious names act.

Partnerships can either be general or limited. Depending on which one it is they may have to file under the Limited Partnership Act, for example. The disadvantages again is that they will both have unlimited liability. Both will be personally and individually liable for all debts and obligations of the partnership. If Mary files for personal bankruptcy and decides to leave the partnership and they owe First Union Bank $10,000, the bank will have recourse to any one of them in trying to satisfy the debt. This is true even if Bob was the only one who signed for the loan originally.

Corporations

A corporation is a business organization that is recognized by law as a separate entity. It does not become one with its owners. It has LIMITED liability. If the owner(s) file for bankruptcy, creditors can only satisfy their claims from the assets of the corporation. Because it is a separate entity recognized by law, it will have to be registered with the state in which it is formed. The owner(s) will have to file an "Articles of Incorporation" describing its purpose and who the owners are.

The advantages of the corporation obviously are that it has limited liability. It is also an organization that can issue shares of stock or bonds in order to finance its needs. Investors who purchase these shares of stock are actually the owners of the corporation. This allows the corporation to have many owners and raise a substantial amount of capital in the process. A corporation is run by a Board of Directors appointed by the owners. The board manages the affairs of the corporation and they work to the best interest of the investors who own the company.

The Accounting Equation

Accounting is based on a simple equation that serves as the fundamental basis of the accounting system. Assets equal liabilities plus owner's equity:

$$A = L + OE$$

This is an important equation that you will need to keep in the back of your mind as you study accounting and as you work in the field. It simply says that the amount that a company owes, added to the owner's equity in the company equals the total Assets that the company has.

Assets

Assets are what a company owns that has an immediate or future value. For example: Cash, accounts receivable (money that the customers owe), equipment etc. Assets can be classified as current or non-current. Current assets are those that will normally be converted into cash or whose benefits are expected to be used up within one year. Cash is the most liquid and is considered to be a current asset. Accounts receivables (A/R) will normally be converted—that is customers will be expected to pay the money they owe in less than a year and so it would be classified as a current asset. A prepaid expense is one where the company pays a sum of money in return for future benefits. For example rent can be paid in advance. When this happens, a current asset is created and the company has the legal right to occupy the space for the period that has been paid in advance.

Non-current assets include assets like equipment (trucks, buildings, machinery…) that have a lifespan of 12 months or more. These assets normally stay on the books longer and are depreciated over their useful lives. We will talk more about depreciation as we go along. For the time being it is simply a way of recovering the cost of the asset over time. If a construction company owns a truck that it uses in the business for the production of income, it is allowed to recover the loss in value of that truck to compensate for the revenue that the asset produces. This is known as <u>depreciation expense.</u>

Liabilities

Liabilities are obligations that a company has. Like assets, they can be classified as <u>current and non-current</u>. Accounts payable (A/P) represents money that a company owes its vendors. When a company purchases raw food to be processed and then sold again to customers, the vendors who sell the raw food are entitled to collect money for their merchandise. A/P like A/R is classified as current because it is expected to be settled in less than one year. When an employee works for a company and they are owed money, another current liability is created know as <u>payroll payable.</u>

Owner's Equity

When you take all the assets of a company and subtract from it all the liabilities, what you have left is the net worth or equity of the owner. You can think of it also on a personal level. An individual has a house, a car, jewelry, furniture and maybe a boat. These are his or her assets. However, the house may carry a mortgage (liability). The car may have a note on which they make monthly payments (liability). Adding up the value of the entire individual's assets and reducing them by the amounts they owe on them, you are left with the net worth—that is the monetary value. They can cash in that monetary value at any time for cash because the net worth is the value they possess.

The same idea holds true in a company. The assets minus what the company owes on them equal the net worth or equity of the owner. In a partnership, each partner would have his own individual equity account. This would keep track of their net worth. In a corporation, this account is known as <u>Stockholders' Equity.</u> This is so because in a corporation, the investors are really the owners.

Debits & Credits

Looking at the accounting equation we just discussed, it is necessary that the equation always be in balance. Accountants speak in terms of debits and credits. You will have to spend some time practicing this a bit, because it may not always sink in right away. Normally we think in terms of debits as subtraction and credits as

Dantes Joseph Jr.

addition. When you receive your bank statement that shows a debit in your checking account, you know that the bank took money away from your account for service fees, for example. Sometimes you may have allowed a creditor to take money out of your account on a regular basis. When this happens your account is being <u>debited</u>. Likewise, when a credit goes through your statement, money is being added back to your account.

Accountants speak a different language when it comes to debits and credits. Debits may increase or decrease an account depending on the type of account it is. Likewise credits may increase or decrease an account depending on the account. Debits will increase an asset account and credits will decrease it. Debits will decrease a liability account and credits will increase it; and the same holds true for the equity account. In summary debits and credits work in the same way we know it with the exception of assets: there it's the opposite. This equation looks something like this:

Account Relationships

Assets	=	Liabilities	+	Equities	
Debit	Credit	Debit	Credit	Debit	Credit
+	-	-	+	-	+
Increase	Decrease	Decrease	Increase	Decrease	Increase

When we talk about Income and expenses in accounting, we are also talking in terms of debits and credits. Income is the revenue that a company generates. A company is in the business to make money unless it is a not-for-profit company. Therefore, the money that it generates from its activities is called sales, revenue or income. The company also encounters some expenses in connection with the income: It has to pay its employees otherwise the company could not exist. It has to put gas in its vehicles in order for them to continue to run. So you can see that you really can't have income without having related expenses. The goal of the company, of course, is to maximize its income (make higher) and minimize the expenses (make lower) in order to show a profit (the excess of revenue over expenses).

When it comes to recording transactions, debits will always increase expenses and credits will decrease them. On the other hand, credits will increase income and debits will decrease it.

Cash vs. Accrual Accounting

Generally all businesses need to choose between the cash or accrual method of accounting. The main difference between the two is keeping track of a business's income and expenses: cash method and accrual method (sometimes called cash basis and accrual basis). In a nutshell, these methods differ only in the timing of when transactions-both sales and purchases are credited or debited to your accounts. If you use the cash method, income is counted when cash (or a check) is physically received and expenses are counted when physically paid. The accrual method is more common. Under this method, transactions are counted when they <u>happen</u> regardless of when the money is actually received or paid. Income is counted when the sale occurs, and expenses are counted when the goods or services are actually received. You don't have to wait until you see the money, or until you actually pay money out of your bank account.

With some transactions, it's not so easy to know when the sale or purchase has occurred. The key date is the <u>job completion date</u>. You can only record the income in your books when you finish a service or deliver all the goods a contract calls for. If a job is mostly completed but will take another 30 days to add the finishing touches, it doesn't go on your books until the 30 days pass. Let's suppose you purchase a computer on credit in March and pay $1,200 for it in May, two months later. Under the cash method of accounting you would record a $1,200 payment for the month of May, the month when the money is actually paid. However under the accrual method, the $1,200 payment would be recorded in March, when you take the computer and are obligated to pay for it. Likewise, if your computer installation business finishes a job on October 31, 2001, and doesn't get paid until January 15, 2002, you'd record the payment in January 2002 under the cash method. Under the accrual method the income would be recorded in your books in October 2001.

In this book we will be using the accrual method of accounting. Revenues and expenses will be deemed to have incurred at the time they are recognized, as discussed above. This method is widely used and is more acceptable because it reflects a more accurate picture of a company's operations and financial position. For the most part, only small businesses, what we would call "mom and pa" operations would use the cash basis.

Tax Years and Accounting Periods

Income and expenses must be reported to the Internal Revenue Service (IRS) for a specific period, called your tax year, accounting period or your fiscal year. The calendar year will have to be used (Jan. 1 to Dec. 31) unless you can substantiate a business reason to use a different period or unless your business is a corporation. Most business owners use the calendar year for their tax year, because it's easy to use. If you want to use a different period, you must request permission from the IRS. Also, your fiscal year must begin on the first day of a month and end on the last day of the month the following year.

The double entry accounting system

The double entry accounting system is a method by which accounting transactions are recorded. The theory is that every transaction always affects at least two different accounts. If XYZ Company spends $50 on advertising, for example, its cash has been reduced (credited) by $50 and also it has created an expense (advertising) for $50 (debit). The typical entry would be as follows:

Advertising expense (increases - debit)..............$50
Cash (decreases - credit).....................................$50

Another example would be that XYZ Company sells 500 widgets at $2 each. This totals $1,000. The cash account increases by $1,000 and yes, the company recognizes income for the same amount. The entry to reflect this is as follows:

Cash (increases—debit).....................................$1,000
Sales (increases—credit)...................................$1,000

You will get more practice on this as we go along. You can already see how the double entry accounting system is set up. This is the whole concept of accounting. You will need to think "double entry" throughout your accounting career.

The Matching Principle Concept

Accountants are expected to match expenses against the income that they generate in the year or period in which they occur. A salesperson commission cannot be recorded on January 31 of one year with the related sales recorded on December 31 of the previous year. Any expense that can be traced to its income should accompany the income in the same period in which they are incurred. Some general expenses however cannot be tied to particular revenue and therefore should be recorded as they occur. An example of this may be advertising expense, repairs and maintenance and some general overhead.

What is an account?

Well you heard me talk about an account and are probably wondering what an account is. In accounting, an account is the device that is used to record and accumulate individual transactions. A transaction is the exchange of value between a business and another entity. The examples we looked at above are transactions. When the company paid $50, it was paid to another company in exchange for a particular service; in this case the other company was to provide advertising services that would eventually benefit XYZ Company. Some asset accounts include the following:

- Cash
- Bank accounts (operational checking account)
- Marketable securities (current investment in stocks, bonds etc…)
- Accounts receivable
- Inventory (the value of merchandise held for resale)
- Prepaid expenses (the current value of future benefits)
- Intangibles (assets such as goodwill or other intangible rights)
- Land and land improvements
- Buildings
- Office equipment
- Vehicles

Some liability accounts include the following:

- Accounts payable
- Payroll payable
- Interest payable (on a loan…)
- Short-term notes payable
- Long-term debt
- Unearned revenue (money received in advance and not yet earned)

Marketable Securities

Marketable securities are short-term investments that a company holds like stocks, bonds, mutual funds etc. They normally will be reported on the balance sheet at the lower of cost or market (LCM). In order for the company to be conservative and not deceive potential investors, it will report the cost (if lower than market) and the market value (if lower than the cost) at the time financials statements are being prepared.

Companies will invest in these short-term securities in order to maximize revenue. If a company has a large amount of cash on hand, it is preferable to invest in short-term securities in order to capitalize on the return they will provide. These returns are generally higher than the interest rate a bank will provide on the funds. Smart managers will study the market in order to decide where to invest excess funds that the company has.

Intangible assets

Intangible assets are assets having a life of one year or more and which lack physical substance (e.g., goodwill) or represent a right granted by the government (e.g., patent) or by another company (like franchise fee). Goodwill is not identifiable. It is internally created. It is the good name and reputation that a company has developed for itself over the years like McDonalds and Burger King. If one were to buy these companies out, you would not only pay for its equipments and fixed assets, you would also pay for the faithful customers that the companies have developed over the years. Intangible assets are amortized (spread out) over the period they benefit using the straight-line method, not to exceed 40 years.

T- accounts

T-accounts are tools used by accountants to quickly analyze the effects of transactions to a particular account. Debits and credits are posted to an account in the form of a "T" to obtain the balance in the account after all elements of the transaction have been taken into consideration. A typical T-account would look like the following:

Accounts Receivable

Debit	Credit
Credit sales 12/1 $500 Credit sales 12/15 350	$700 Payments received 12/28
Balance 12/31 $150	

Contra-Asset Accounts

Contra-asset accounts are used to measure the declination or reduction in value or potential value of a particular account. One such account is **"Allowance for bad debts."** This account has a normal credit balance and is used with "Accounts Receivable." In order to understand this we need to take a closer look at Accounts Receivable. This account simply represents the amount of money that is owed a company in connection with credit sales extended to its customers. Think about your own credit card accounts. Some company extended credit to you and has an account in their books called "Accounts Receivable" because you are their customer and they are in the business of lending money. Do you think that these companies always collect the amount they have showing in that account? You may lose your job, file bankruptcy or die. Somewhere along the line the company is not going to be able to collect some of the money they have out there.

In order to show a conservative account—that is one that will not mislead readers of the financial statements, the company has to adjust the "Accounts Receivable" account to show a possible amount that is not collectible. This is called "Bad Debts". These are debts that the company will never collect. It's a cost of doing business. Assuming XYZ company shows total accounts receivable at 12/31/01 of $25,700 and management decides, from prior year trends and past experience, that 5% of that amount the company will never see even if they hire a collection agency to go after the delinquent customers. The journal entry to record this would look like the following:

Bad debt expense at 12/31/01 ($25,700 x 5%)..........$1,285
Allowance for bad debts $1,285
To record expected uncollectible accounts at year-end.

Notice that the account "Bad debt expense" is debited (increased). This would be the account affected in the double entry accounting system. The Accounts receivable account would appear on the financial statements (balance sheet) as follows:

Cash	$5,000
Bank account	36,000
Marketable securities	10,000
Accounts Receivable	
(Net of allowance for bad debts of $1,285)	24,415

Different companies may disclose this in different ways, but the general idea is to show the <u>net amount</u> as the final receivable from the customers.

Another contra account is "Accumulated Depreciation". Depreciation is discussed a little bit later in this chapter. What you have to realize is that depreciation is to reduce the value of a fixed asset. Fixed assets are recorded at cost and will always appear on the balance sheet at cost. However, over time the fixed assets go down in value and therefore, that reduction must be reflected in the account. Consider the following entry to record depreciation on a certain asset:

Depreciation expense at 12/31/01 ....$1,500
Accumulated depreciation $1,500

To record depreciation on fixed assets at the end of the year.

Assuming a fixed asset balance, before depreciation, of $18,000, the fixed asset may appear on the balance sheet as follows:

Cash	$5,000
Bank account	36,000
Marketable securities	10,000
Accounts Receivable	
(Net of allowance for bad debts of $1,285)	24,415
Fixed assets (net of accumulated	
depreciation of $1,500)	16,500

There are some other contra accounts that you will come across, but these are the most common. They are not difficult to follow. Once you understand the logic behind these contra accounts, you will understand how they are used with other accounts.

Bank Reconciliation

Have you ever tried to reconcile your checking account? Every one of us I think to some degree has. The fact is that most people find it frustrating and they may give up after a few minutes. As an accountant this is one of the most common things you will be called on to do. Whether you reconcile a personal or a business account, the concept is the same. If you keep in mind the logic of what it is that you are trying to do, then you will find the process relatively easy.

In bank reconciliation, you are trying to identify the "reconciling items" that exist between your book balance and your bank balance as of a <u>specific date</u>. By "reconciling items," I mean the checks that have been written that have not yet been cashed or processed by the bank (outstanding checks) and the deposits that have been made and that are not yet reflected in the bank statement (deposits in transit). Obviously there has to be a bookkeeping, whether personal or business, that is maintained constantly; checks are written, deposits are made etc. The bank that pays your checks and receives the deposits you make also is keeping your books. However, the timing is altogether different. The difference that exists between the bank and the book balance are referred to as "timing differences;" that is it's only a matter of time before both books reflect the same entries.

Other items that may affect the differences in the two book balances are service fees that the bank will charge, errors that may occur in the company's books or in the bank's books and other miscellaneous debit and credit memos. It is important to keep in mind that the reconciliation is done <u>as of</u> a specific date. In other words you are trying to determine why exactly there is a difference between the two books as of 12/31/01 for example. Consider the following:

XYZ Company shows a book balance of $12,500 as of 12/31/01. When the company receives the bank statement on January 7, 2002 it shows that the bank balance as of 12/31/01 was $14,368. A review of the checkbook reveals that check numbers 1020 for $1,325 and check 1021 for $1,540 were written on 12/27/01. In addition the company deposited $1,000 on 12/30/01. You also notice that check # 1015 that was issued for rent was erroneously posted in the checkbook for $864 when it should have been for $846. The bank has it correct on the bank statement. In addition the bank charged the company $15 for its services.

In order to reconcile these two books we must prepare a well-labeled computation sheet that will make things easier for us to see. The following is what the reconciliation would look like:

Book balance as of 12/31/01		**$12,500**
Add: Outstanding checks #1020 & 1021 ($1,325 + $1,540)	$2,865	
Error in recording #1015 ($864—$846)	18	2,883
Less: Deposits in transit	$1,000	
Bank service fees	15	<1,015>
Bank balance as of 12/31/01		**$14,368**

Notice that when check #1015 was recorded in error the company took out an additional $18 too much from the books. This money has to be added back in order to come in line with the bank balance.

Generally outstanding checks (O/S) are added to the book balance and deposits in transits (DIT) are deducted. Here we reconciled from the book to the bank balance. You can also reverse it and start with the bank balance to reconcile to the books. In doing so outstanding checks would be subtracted from the bank balance because the bank hasn't processed these checks yet, but they have been recorded on the books. Likewise deposits in transit would have to be added to the bank balance because it's already reflected on the books. Some common sense and good logic are the key ingredients to reconciling a bank account.

Another way of looking at bank reconciliation is to look at both books. Entries that appear on both books need not be reconciled. It's only items that appear on one and not the other or vice-versa that you need to analyze and adjust.

Adjusting entries: Once you've reconciled the account, you need to bring the books up to date by recording the related reconciling items. The journal entries that you would make are the following:

Bank account $18
Rent expense...$18
To adjust books and rent expense recorded in error

Bank fees expense...$15
Bank account $15
To record bank service fees for the month of December 2001.

Notice that no entries are necessary for the outstanding checks nor the deposit in transit. These are <u>timing differences</u> and will adjust themselves eventually when the bank processes the transactions.

Inventory

Inventory is the merchandise that is held by a company for sale to the general public. It is a current asset because it is one that the company expects to sell in the immediate future. Inventory is not normally held for periods of more than 12 months. This account is normally reported at <u>cost</u> on the Balance Sheet (See chapter 6). In this book we will look at four different methods of valuing inventory:

Dantes Joseph Jr.

    Cost—This method reports the exact amount paid for merchandise purchased, adjusted by shipping (freight) and other costs required to purchase the merchandise. This is often called the <u>Specific Identification Method</u>. Consider the following example:

    XYZ Company prepared a purchase order to buy 1500 widgets from ABC Company at $1.50 per widget. ABC charged an extra $75 for shipping. The total value of the widgets is $2,325.00 (1500 x $1.5 + $75). On the Balance sheet, $2,325.00 would be shown as inventory if the widgets were still on hand at the end of the year. Although widgets are used as an example here, the specific identification method is normally used with high ticket or large inventory items like automobiles, furniture, jewelry etc.

    Fist in first out (FIFO)—This method of valuing inventory says that the oldest (first in) unit cost of inventory items purchased is the first to be used as the cost of the items being sold by the company. The following transactions relate to XYZ Company:

    11/02/01 XYZ Company purchased the 1500 widgets at $1.50 a piece

    11/15/01 the company buys an additional 1200 widgets at 1.65 per widget

    12/17/01 the company buys again 1000 widgets at 1.75 a piece

    12/21/01 the company sells 2000 widgets for a profit at $3.75 per unit

    12/27/01 the company sells again 900 widgets for $3.75 per unit.

What is the ending inventory value under the FIFO method? The following chart should serve to simplify the problem.

Date	Quantity	Unit cost	Purchases (A/P)	Cost of Sales (Inventory)	Cumulative Inventory Unit bal.	Cumulative Inventory Value
11/02/01	1500	1.50	$2,250		1500	$2,250
11/15/01	1200	1.65	1,980		2700	4,230
12/17/01	1000	1.75	1,750		3700	5,980
12/21/01	-1500	1.50		2,250	2200	3,730
12/21/01	-500	1.65		825	1700	2,905
12/27/01	-700	1.65		1,155	1000	1,750
12/27/01	-200	1.75		350	800	1,400
Totals	800		$5,980		$4,580	

A couple of things to notice in this grid: even though 2000 widgets were sold on 12/21/01, only 1500 is being valued at $1.50 because that's the total we have in inventory that was purchased at that price. The difference of 500 has to be valued at the unit cost from the next batch of 1200 that was bought at $1.65 a piece. The same applies for the next sale etc. You work your way through the batches that were purchased and use the appropriate unit cost to assign to the units that are being sold. $1,400 would be your inventory value at 12/31/01. Once your grid is complete then journalizing these transactions become easy and they would be recorded as follows:

Purchases $5,980
Accounts payable...$5,980
To record purchases of 3700 widgets from 11/2 to 12/17/01

Account receivable $10,875
Sales (2000 + 900 x $3.75)............................$10,875
To record the sale of 2900 widgets from 12/21 to 12/27

When a company records sales it is usually accompanied by an entry to record the cost of sales or cost of goods sold. Remember we talked about the Matching Principle Concept; revenues always have to be matched to its related costs. In this particular case it would be what the company paid for these widgets versus what they were sold for.

Dantes Joseph Jr.

The difference between the two is the profit the company gets to keep. The related entry would be as follows:

Cost of goods sold..$4,580
Inventory... $4,580
To record the cost of goods sold on the sale of 2900 widgets

The above entry is made when a company keeps a running record of the inventory it has on hand. This is known as a <u>Perpetual Inventory System (PIS).</u> A physical inventory is usually taken from time to time or at the end of the year, depending on the company and the type of inventory that it carries. With a PIS the company has a good idea of the balance of its inventory account at all times. The company may still decide to count its inventory at the end of the year in order to adjust any differences that may arise do to theft, fire or other factors.

Last in first out (LIFO)—This method of valuing inventory says that the most recent (last in) unit cost of inventory items purchased is the first to be used (first out) as the cost of the items being sold by the company. Using the above example we would obtain the following results:

11/02/01 XYZ Company purchased the 1500 widgets at $1.50 a piece
11/15/01 the company buys an additional 1200 widgets at 1.65 per widget
12/17/01 the company buys again 1000 widgets at 1.75 a piece
12/21/01 the company sells 2000 widgets for a profit at $3.75 per unit
12/27/01 the company sells again 900 widgets for $3.75 per unit.

Date	Quantity	Unit cost	Purchases (A/P)	Cost of Sales (Inventory)	Cumulative Inventory Unit bal.	Cumulative Inventory Value
11/02/01	1500	1.50	$2.250		1500	$2,250
11/15/01	1200	1.65	1.980		2700	4,230
12/17/01	1000	1.75	1.750		3700	5,980
12/21/01	-1000	1.75		$1,750	2700	4,230
12/21/01	-1000	1.65		1,650	1700	2,580
12/27/01	-200	1.65		330	1500	2,250
12/27/01	-700	1.50		1,050	800	$1,200
Totals	800		$5,980	$4,780		

A couple of things to notice in this grid: even though 2000 widgets were sold on 12/21/01, only 1000 is being valued at $1.75 because that's the total we have in inventory that were purchased at that price. The difference of 1000 has to be valued at the unit cost from the next batch of 1200 that was bought at $1.65 a piece. The same applies for the next sale etc. $1,200 would be your inventory value at 12/31/01. Once your grid is complete then journalizing these transactions become easy and they would be recorded as follows:

```
Purchases ..........................................$5,980
Accounts payable..................................$5,980
To record purchases of 3700 widgets from 11/2 to 12/17/01

Accounts receivable..............................$10,875
Sales (2000 + 900 x $3.75)....................$10,875
To record the sale of 2900 widgets from 12/21 to 12/27

Cost of goods sold ..............................$4,780
Inventory..............................................$4,780
To record the cost of goods sold on the sale of 2900 widgets
```

Weighted Average—This method of valuing inventory takes into account the weighted average of the unit costs of all the merchandise purchased. Using the above example we would obtain the following results:

11/02/01 XYZ Company purchased the 1500 widgets at $1.50 a piece

11/15/01 the company buys an additional 1200 widgets at 1.65 per widget

12/17/01 the company buys again 1000 widgets at 1.75 a piece

12/21/01 the company sells 2000 widgets for a profit at $3.75 per unit

12/27/01 the company sells again 900 widgets for $3.75 per unit.

Date	Quantity	Unit cost	Purchases (A/P)	Cost of Sales (Inventory)	Cumulative Inventory Unit bal.	Cumulative Inventory Value
11/02/01	1500	1.50	$2,250		1500	$2,250
11/15/01	1200	1.65	1,980		2700	4,230
12/17/01	1000	1.75	1,750		3700	5,980
Weighted	Average	1.63				
12/21/01	-2000	1.63		$3,260	1700	2,720
12/27/01	-900	1.63		1,467	800	$1,253
Totals	800		$5,980	$4,727		

Things to notice in this grid: all 2900 widgets sold, are valued at the weighted average cost of $1.63. This method takes the inflation factor that causes the rise in the cost of merchandise and uniformly spreads it out over the cost of goods sold. $1,253 would be your inventory value at 12/31/01 in this example. Once your grid is complete then journalizing these transactions become easy and they would be recorded as follows:

Purchases...$5,980
Accounts payable.. $5,980
To record purchases of 3700 widgets from 11/2 to 12/17/01

Accounts receivable...$10,875
Sales (2000 + 900 x $3.75)... $10,875
To record the sale of 2900 widgets from 12/21 to 12/27

Cost of goods sold..$4,727
Inventory... $4,727
To record the cost of goods sold on the sale of 2900 widgets

Following is a global view of three of the methods we've discussed and how they affect cost of goods sold and ending inventory:

	FIFO	LIFO	Weighted Average
Sales	$10,875	$10,875	$10,875
Cost of goods sold	4,580	4,780	4,727
Gross profit:	$6,295	$6,095	$6,148
Ending Inventory	$1,400	$1,200	$1,253

It is interesting to see the inverse relationship here with the different methods of valuing inventory. The FIFO method will always yield a lower cost of goods sold with a higher ending inventory. This is true because the oldest (lower) unit costs are being used with the goods sold, and the ending inventory is receiving the more recent (higher) unit costs for the merchandise on hand.

The opposite is true with the LIFO method. A higher cost of goods sold results because the more recent (higher) unit costs are being applied to the items being sold and the oldest (lower) unit costs are being applied to the ending inventory.

The weighted average method is spreading all the unit costs over the merchandise sold and therefore the cost of goods sold will still be higher than the FIFO method and slightly lower than the LIFO. The ending inventory here also is slightly higher. This may vary with different examples depending on the range to which these prices fluctuate.

Calculating the Cost of Goods Sold

Cost of goods sold is just what the name implies. It is the cost a company pays for the merchandise that it sells. Since we have to match revenues with expenses, it is important that we accurately calculate what that cost is. So far we have been assuming a perpetual inventory system where the journal entry is made at the time merchandise is sold to adjust the level of inventory on hand.

Most companies use a <u>Periodic Inventory System</u>. This is where a running total of inventory is not kept. Rather, at the time that a company is preparing its financial reports, it will analyze the cost of goods sold in the body of the report or as a separate disclosure elsewhere in the report. Let us expand a little bit on the example we used earlier under the Cost Method of valuing inventory:

XYZ Company prepared a purchase order to buy 1500 widgets from ABC Company at $1.50 per widget. ABC charged an extra $75 for shipping the merchandise. The total value of the widgets is $2,325.00 (1500 x $1.5 + $75). Let us also assume that the company returned 200 bad widgets 3 days later. The beginning inventory on the books was $12,575 and the ending inventory is $7,800. An analysis of the sales journal reveals that the company sold $25,000 worth of widgets over the same accounting period. Cost of goods sold would be determined as follows:

Sales			$25,000
Cost of goods sold			
Beginning inventory	$12,575		
Purchase (1500 x 1.50)	2,250		
Freight (shipping)	75		
Less: returns and allowances (200 x 1.50)	-300		
Total goods available for sale		14,600	
Less: ending inventory		-7,800	$6,800
Total Gross Profit			**$18,200**

The idea is to start with your opening inventory; this is last year's closing inventory that was on the company's books. Next you want to add to that, the purchases that occurred for the period and adjusting that for returns and freight associated with the purchase. You are then left with the <u>total goods available for sale</u>. In the space of 3 months, for example this is the total merchandise that the company had at its disposition to sell to the public. The difference between that figure and the ending inventory is the cost of goods sold; the actual cost of the merchandise to the company.

It is obvious to see that this method of calculating cost of sales (another name for cost of goods sold) does not take into account the FIFO, LIFO or weighted average methods discussed earlier.

Office Supplies

This account is one that requires a little bit of attention because of the two ways in which it can be treated on the balance sheet. Office supplies are the necessities in an office such as pens, paper, glue, folders, clipboards, staplers, 2 hole punches etc. If a company were in the business of buying these items to sell for a profit, most of it would be considered inventory and therefore treated as such. Even a company like that, however, would still have these items in their offices that would still come under the category of "supplies".

Office supplies can either be capitalized—that is recorded <u>as an asset</u> when it is purchased and then adjusted at year-end to recognize the portion that has been used as <u>expense</u>. The other method of treatment is to record the purchases as expenses and then adjust the account at the end of the year to recognize the asset. In order to adjust the account at year-end, a physical inventory of the supplies would be taken to determine the quantity on hand.

Recording the expense—XYZ Company buys $75 of supplies on June 6, 2001. On November 21 of the same year it bought an additional $87 of supplies. On December 31, 2001 when the company is ready to close the year and prepare its financial statements, it counted the supplies on hand and recorded a value $52. Using a T-account as discussed earlier, the scenario would look like this:

Office Supplies (asset)

Debit	Credit
Purchase 6/6/01 $75 Purchase 11/21/01 87 **Balance 12/31 $52**	$110 Supplies used (expense)

Dantes Joseph Jr.

Notice that by using the T-account you can plug in the numbers you know to back into the amount that you are looking for. In this case, the $110 expense the company incurred. This would be the monetary amount of used paper, ink, white out etc. The journal entries to record these transactions are as follows:

6/6/01 Office supplies...$75
11/21/01 Office supplies...$87
Cash...$162
To record the purchase of office supplies in June and November, 2001

12/31/01 Supplies expense....................................$110
Office supplies $110
To record office supplies expense from 6/6/01 to 12/31/01

Recording the asset—If the purchases are not recorded in the asset account, it will be put directly into the expense account at the time the purchase is made. If this were the case, the inventory of supplies on hand would still be taken at the end of the year in order to determine the monetary value to assign to the asset. The T-account and journal entries would look something like this:

Supplies Expense

Debit	Credit
Purchase 6/6/01 $75 Purchase 11/21/01 87	$52 Supplies Remaining (asset) **12/31/01**
Balance 12/31/01 $110	

6/6/01 Supplies expense...................................$75
11/21/01 Supplies expense...............................$87
Cash.. $162
To record the purchase of office supplies in June and November, 2001

30

12/31/01 Office supplies...$52
Supplies expense...$52
To record office supplies asset at 12/31/01

In the real world only very large companies whose office supplies would represent a sizable amount on their financial statements would record the purchase of supplies as asset. Most small companies would not even bother. They simply record an expense every time they buy office supplies. As an accountant, you will have to use your own judgment to determine how you want to classify these purchases.

Petty Cash

This is an area that can appear relatively simple and yet be somewhat complex. Usually most disbursements in a company are in the form of a check. Checks are used to pay for office supplies, inventory, and pay other bills and employees. However, some cash is normally kept on hand by the bookkeeper or a clerk. This cash is kept in a safe and is known as "Petty Cash". It is an asset and is shown on the Balance Sheet as "cash" or "petty cash". This money is used to pay for small items like stamps, flowers for special occasions and gas or toll for certain employees. It is used for anything and everything that you can think of where a check would not be necessary or appropriate. An employee may run to a local store to buy some napkins or other miscellaneous items that the company needs right away. The money would come out of that account. The person who wants the money would sign for it on a petty-cash receipt. The receipt is pretty straightforward and shows the amount, the purpose of the disbursement and space for the signature of the one taking out the cash. There may also be a space for the approval of a manager if the nature of the disbursement requires it. Normally most petty cash disbursements are routine and may not require special approval.

Depending on the size of the company and the frequency of petty-cash activity, management would decide just how much money should be kept in that account. Let us assume right now a petty-cash account of $500. The total of all receipts and cash left in the box should always total $500. The person handling that account maybe held liable for any discrepancies that arise. When the account is running low, the bookkeeper or whoever is handling it will ask that the account be replenished. This is done by recording all the expenses (receipts) from the box through an entry. Consider the following example:

Original set up of the petty-cash account:

Petty Cash (increase—debit)...$500
Example Bank (decrease—credit) $500
To establish a petty-cash account in the amount of $500.

After three months, we notice the following receipts in the box:

Flowers & cards $55.00
Miscellaneous supplies 45.00
Expense reimbursement to an employee.............................62.50
Cash paid to a computer consultant
(independent contractor) 150.00
Stamps purchased...34.00
Cash advance to a manager for a 1-day seminar................<u>125.00</u>
    Total   <u>$471.50</u>

Cash found is in the amount of $28.50. This totals the $500 petty-cash account. The bookkeeper then decides to have the account replenished. This means that the company needs to write a check, payable to "Petty Cash" for $471.50. A trusted messenger will take that check to the bank, cash it and bring the money to the person handling the petty-cash account so it can go in the safe.

The entry to replenish petty cash:

Office expense (increase—debit)..$55.00
Supplies expense (increase—debit) 45.00
Meals & Entertainment (increase—debit) 62.50
Miscellaneous labor (increase—debit) 150.00
Postage (increase—debit) 34.00
Employee advances (increase—debit).................................125.00
Example Bank (decrease—credit) $471.50

To replenish the petty-cash account.

The employee advance of $125 is an asset account. It's considered a loan until the manager returns with receipts showing how the money was spent. At that time the expenses will be recorded and the advance account will be credited. All other debits are made to the related expense accounts. Finally the bank account is reduced through the check written to replenish the account. This would bring that account back up to $500.

The important thing to keep in mind here is that the petty-cash account is only debited when it is originally set up. It is not credited when replenished. Rather the expenses are recorded in the General Journal (discussed in chapter 4) and the check cashed and deposited right back into the petty cash box as if it were never spent. Thus the petty-cash account would still reflect a balance of $500.

Depreciation Expense

Earlier we talked briefly about depreciation and fixed assets. Long-term assets are those whose useful lives are more than one year. Their useful lives have to be estimated and depreciated over time. Depreciation is simply the allocation of the cost of an asset over its useful life. Remember in the matching principle concept, we have to match revenues with the related expenses. If machinery is producing paper plates, for example, the plates are expected to be sold and generate revenue. However, the machine that's making the plates is also depreciating (going down in value). This is why we need to recognize that expense from the asset in order to properly match the two. Typically most assets that are depreciated can be expected to be salvaged for some amount of cash at the end of its useful life. This is known as Salvage Value.

Fixed assets include buildings, machinery and equipment, office equipment such as copiers, computers, printers etc. Land is never depreciated because its value does not depreciate. If anything it tends to go up in value rather than down. In this study we will look at the main depreciation methods used. We'll see how they are calculated and how they differ from one another.

Straight Line Depreciation—This is the most common method of calculating depreciation. It assumes that the asset will decrease in value evenly over its useful life. Buildings and improvements are one example of such assets. The formula to calculate straight-line depreciation is as follows:

$$\text{Depreciation expense} = \frac{\text{Total cost—salvage value}}{\text{Estimated useful life}}$$

Keep in mind that the cost of the asset will include not only the amount paid for it, but also <u>all necessary</u> costs incurred in bringing the asset to a point where it can be place into operation. These would include sales tax, shipping, storage, test runs etc.

Double Declining Balance (DDB)—this is an accelerated depreciation method mostly used when the productivity of an asset is expected to be greater in the early years of use.

Certain types of machinery and equipment that usually produce the most early on in their useful lives will fit into this category. Depreciation is highest early on and then dramatically declines over the years. The formula for the DDB is as follows:

$$\text{Depreciation expense} = 2 \text{ x } \frac{1}{\text{Estimated useful life}} \text{ x book value at the beginning of the year}$$

Sum Of The Year's Digits (SYD)—Like the DDB, the SYD is another form of accelerated depreciation that assumes that a fixed asset loses a greater portion of its value in the early years of use. It's a less accelerated method than the DDB, however the idea is the same. Certain trucks and other vehicles are more efficiently productive in the initial years of use and are good candidates for this method. The formula is a little more complex than the DDB, but the outcome is similar:

$$\text{Depreciation expense} = \text{Cost—salvage value X applicable fraction}$$

$$\text{Applicable fraction} = \frac{\text{Remaining useful life at beginning of the year}}{\text{SYD}}$$

$$\text{SYD} = \frac{n(n+1)}{2}$$

Where "n" is equal to the estimated useful life of the asset.

Units of Production (UOP)—This method allocates depreciation expense based on actual physical usage. Assets with uncertain useful lives and limited productive capacity fit well into this category. A piece of machinery may be good for 20,000 hours of use, for example but the useful life of the asset is not certain. It may take 5, 8 or even 12 years to produce these 20,000 hours. Furthermore, the use of the hours is not evenly spread. It may produce 5,000 the first year and only sporadically over the next couple of years.

The UOP, therefore helps spread the life of the asset over the period in which it is most productive.

The systematic estimate of the number of units an asset will produce is required by generally accepted accounting principles (GAAP) whether it is miles, hours or some other unit of measure. The formula to calculate this method is as follows:

Depreciation expense = Units produced for the year X UOP rate

UOP rate =   Cost—salvage value
Total estimated units to be produced over the useful life

Notice that this method only calculates the UOP rate. When the total number of units is produced and is known, it has to be multiplied by the rate to come up with the depreciation expense for that period.

The following example shows a chart with 3 different types of depreciation methods: straight line, DDB and the SYD. The example depreciates only one asset (Kitchen Freezer) under all 3 depreciation methods so you will see the difference between the individual methods. The asset assumes a 15-year useful life and a cost of $25,000 with a salvage value of $2,500.

This example may not be realistic, but it is simply for illustrative purposes. The kitchen freezer may have a life of maybe 35 years even. This is done in an effort to save space. The general idea should be clear, however.

XYZ Company
Depreciation Schedule

	Kitchen Freezer (Straight Line)	Kitchen Freezer (SYD)	Kitchen Freezer (DDB)
Date placed in service	01/01/01	01/01/01	01/01/01
Useful Life (years)	15	15	15
Total Cost	$25,000	$25,000	$25,000
Salvage Value	2,500	2,500	2,500
Depreciable base	22,500	22,500	22,500
FY2001	$1,500	$2,812.50	$3,333.33
FY2002	1,500	2,625.00	2,888.89
FY2003	1,500	2,437.50	2,503.70
FY2004	1,500	2,250.00	2,169.88
FY2005	1,500	2,062.50	1,880.56
FY2006	1,500	1,875.00	1,629.82
FY2007	1,500	1,687.50	1,412.51
FY2008	1,500	1,500.00	1,224.17
FY2009	1,500	1,312.50	1,060.95
FY2010	1,500	1,125.00	919.49
FY2011	1,500	937.50	796.89
FY2012	1,500	750.00	690.64
FY2013	1,500	562.50	598.55
FY2014	1,500	375.00	518.75
FY2015	1,500	187.50	449.58*
	22,500	22,500	22,077.71

* The DDB formula does not take into account the salvage value until the very end of the depreciation process. At this stage, the book balance of the asset would be $2,922.29 (25,000—22,077.71).

Because the book value is $2,500, the last year's depreciation would be $872.57 (449.58 + 422.99 (2,922.29—2,500)). Pennies would be rounded into that figure. The figure you would then be left with is the salvage value of the asset, which is $2,500. The asset cannot be depreciated beyond its salvage value.

Amortization Expense

Amortization expense differs from depreciation expense in that it is only used in connection with <u>intangible</u> assets (discussed earlier). Amortization of intangible assets is straight-line method only generally not to exceed 40 years. Unlike depreciation where the debit goes to the depreciation expense and the credit to accumulated depreciation, the debit to amortization is to "amortization expense", but the credit goes directly to the asset (goodwill, patents etc.).

Depletion Expense

Depletion is similar to depreciation except it is used in connection with the measure of production of natural resources such as minerals, oil, gas etc. It is computed by dividing "cost" minus "salvage value" by the estimated total quantity expected to produce over the estimated useful life. The resulting ratio or percentage is multiplied by the production of a given period. The journal entry also is to debit "depletion expense" and credit the asset directly (not a contra account).

Dantes Joseph Jr.

CHAPTER 3

EXERCISE

1. Which of the following is not a form of business organization?

    ○   **A** Corporation

    ◉   **B** Limited liability

    ○   **C** Sole proprietor

    ○   **D** Partnership

2. The following is not an advantage to forming a corporation?

    ◉   **A** Limited liability

    ○   **B** Unlimited liability

    ○   **C** Shares of stock

    ○   **D** Separate entity

3. Which of the following is the correct accounting equation?

    ◉   **A** A = L - OE   _ASSET = LIAbility - Owel Equity_

    ○   **B** A = L + OE

    ○   **C** A = L x OE

    ○   **D** A - L / OE

4. Which of the following is not a characteristic of a current asset?

    ○   **A** 12 months or more

    ○   **B** Short term

    ○   **C** Liquidity

    ○   **D** 12 months or less

5. Which of the following is classified as a short-term liability?

- ○ **A** Accounts receivable
- ○ **B** Cash
- ○ **C** Unearned income
- ○ **D** Goodwill

6. The following account is increased by a debit.

- ● **A** Accounts payable
- ○ **B** Payroll payable
- ○ **C** Goodwill
- ○ **D** Owner's equity

7. Which of the following account is not increased by a credit?

- ○ **A** Owner's equity
- ● **B** Accounts receivable
- ○ **C** Accounts payable
- ○ **D** Sales

8. The following account is decreased by a debit.

- ○ **A** Owner's withdrawal
- ○ **B** Cash
- ○ **C** Accounts receivable
- ○ **D** Goodwill

9. A debit will always increase the cash account.

- ○ **True**
- ○ **False**

10. A credit will always decrease the accounts payable.

Dantes Joseph Jr.

○ **True**

○ **False**

11. The double entry accounting system says that at least 2 accounts will be affected in a journal entry.

○ **True**

◉ **False**

12. The matching principle concept says that your debits should always equal your credits.

○ **True**

○ **False**

13. Which of the following accounts is not classified as a non-current asset?

◉ **A** Machinery & Equipment

○ **B** Inventory

○ **C** Land

○ **D** Office building

14. Which of the following is a long-term liability?

○ **A** Payroll payable

○ **B** Interest payable

○ **C** Bonds payable

○ **D** Unearned income

15. Intangible assets are those that can be converted into cash within a period of 12 months.

○ **True**

○ **False**

16. A contra-asset account will normally carry a credit balance.

○   **True**

○   **False**

17. Which of the following is classified as a contra-asset account?

○   **A** Sales return

○   **B** Accumulated depreciation

○   **C** Purchase discounts

○   **D** Purchase returns

18. In a bank reconciliation, which of the following items need not be adjusted on the books?

○   **A** Deposit in transit

○   **B** Service charges

○   **C** Transposition errors

○   **D** Credit memos

19. A company purchased $22,000 of merchandise during the year; $1,200 of which were returned. An analysis of the sales journal shows sales totaling $65,000. The gross profit has been about 30% of total sales over the past 3 years. If the beginning inventory was $38,000 what is the cost of goods sold and ending inventory calculated at the end of the year?

20. ABC Company had the following information regarding purchases and sales over the year: 6/1/xx Purchased 1000 units @ 1.20/unit 7/10/xx Purchased 1500 units @ 1.50/unit 8/8/xx Sold 500 units @ $3.75/unit 12/20/xx Sold 1200 units @ 3.75/unit Compute the ending inventory and cost of goods sold (total $ amount) under the LIFO valuation method.

21. A company purchased office supplies during the year as follows: 6/1/xx $125 7/10/xx $ 75 12/5/xx $100 On 12/31/xx, a physical inventory count reveals $110 worth of supplies on hand. What is the journal entry to recognize the asset on 12/31/xx if purchases were lumped into the supplies expense account?

22. Which of the following is not an accelerated method of depreciation?

○   **A** ACRS

○   **B** SYD

Dantes Joseph Jr.

○   **C** Straight line

○   **D** DDB

23. Which of the following methods does not take salvage value into consideration in computing depreciation?

○   **A** Units of production

○   **B** DDB

○   **C** SYD

○   **D** ACRS

24. Which of the following expenses uses a contra-asset account in recording cost recovery?

○   **A** Depreciation

○   **B** Amortization

○   **C** Depletion

○   **D** ACRS

25. The FIFO method of valuing inventory will result in a higher cost of goods sold and a lower inventory.

○   **True**

○   **False**

Answer Key:
Chapter 3 exercise

Answer
1 - B
2 - B
3 - B
4 - A
5 - C
6 - C
7 - B
8 - A
9 - TRUE
10 - FALSE
11 - TRUE
12 - FALSE

| 13 - B |
| 14 - C |
| 15 - FALSE |
| 16 - TRUE |
| 17 - B |
| 18 - A |

19

Sales...$65,000

Cost of Goods Sold:
Beginning Inventory 38,000
Add: Purchases..22,000
Less: Total returns & allowances.................................... -1,200
Total Available for sale...58,800

Less: Ending Inventory .... -13,300 45,500
Gross Profit (30% of sales)...$19,500

20

Cost of sales:

500 units @ 1.50	=	$750
1000 @ 1.50	=	1,500
200 @ 1.20	=	240
		$2,490

Ending Inventory:

1000 @ 1.20	=	1,200
1500 @ 1.50	=	2,250
		$3,450
Less: Cost (from above)	-	2,490
Total Ending Inventory		960

Dantes Joseph Jr.

21	

Journal entry to record the asset:

Office Supplies...$110

Supplies Expense $110

To adjust supplies expense and recognize office supplies asset at year end.

22 - C
23 - B
24 - A
25 - FALSE

Chapter 4

Recording transactions and posting To the General Ledger

Source documents

In order to properly record transactions in accounting, we must know the different types of source documents we will be looking at: These are the invoices, receipts, purchase orders, purchase requisitions etc. When a company sells its merchandise, it normally prepares an invoice to give to the customer. The invoice will normally contain an invoice number, a description of the merchandise sold, the price per unit, the total price, the due date and other pertinent information regarding the sale.

When a purchase is initiated in a company, normally an internal document is prepared called a "purchase requisition." The department that wants the merchandise will create this document and turn it into the proper supervisor for approval. Once approved, a purchase order (PO) is created. One copy is sent to the vendor who is to supply the merchandise; another copy is sent to the receiving department awaiting the merchandise to arrive. Upon arrival, the receiving department compares the vendor invoice to the PO to make sure that everything that was ordered is delivered. Finally copies of the vendor invoice, PO and receiving documents are sent to the accounting department for recording. The typical entry to record the purchase (transaction) would look something like this:

Purchases (increase—debit)..............................$1,500
Accounts payable (increase—credit)....................$1,500

Once the invoice is finally paid, the accounting department would record the transaction with the following entry:

Accounts payable (decrease—debit)....................$1,500
Cash (decrease—credit)................................$1,500

The basic concept is that accounting documents, such as the ones mentioned above are usually required before an entry can be recorded. Some entries do not require source document; they are normally called adjusting entries. We will study those in more detail in chapter 5.

Invoice discounts

Vendors who sell their products or merchandise will normally provide an incentive for prompt payment of an invoice. They may offer a 2% discount if the invoice is paid within 10 days. If not, the entire amount will have to be paid in 30 days. A smart accountant will always want to take advantage of these discounts because in the long run they do add up. I have worked for companies where the Chief Financial Officer (CFO) or President does not take advantage of these discounts through prompt payment of the invoices. This usually happens if the accounting system is weak. The invoices are not processed fast enough so as to be approved by a supervisor for payment and so the discount date usually passes and the entire invoice amount has to be paid. It is unfortunate, as I said, because such a company is not really minimizing its expenses to improve its financial statements. Sometimes these discounts are abbreviated as follows:

- 2% 10 net 30 (2% discount if paid within 10 days or full payment in 30 days)
- 3% 10 net 15 (3% discount if paid within 10 days or full payment in 15 days)
- Due on receipt (no discounts extended. The entire amount is due upon receipt of the invoice)
- Net 15 (no discounts extended. The entire invoice amount is due in 15 days).

When a company has a good relationship with a vendor and they've been doing business for some time, most purchases are usually done <u>on account.</u> In other words credit is established where payments on purchases are postponed for at least 30 days. The liability created in connection with the deferral of the payment is called <u>Accounts Payable.</u> (A/P) The opposite is true where the company is on the receiving end. They are called <u>Accounts Receivable</u> (A/R).

The Sales Journal (SJ)

When an invoice is created to record a sale, it is normally recorded in a journal called the <u>Sales Journal.</u> This is where you would expect to find all of the entries on company sales whether or not they were made on account (credit) or cash was received at the time. This journal is pretty straightforward and does not normally include columns for debits and credits. You would expect to find the date the sale was made, the customer's name, the items that were sold, the price, the quantity and finally the extended total dollar amount of the sale. The sales journal can be kept by a bookkeeper or even someone that does not have any knowledge in accounting.

Dantes Joseph Jr.

XYZ Company
Sales Journal

Page 3

Date	Customer	Description	Qty	Unit $	Total
12/14/01	ABC Company	Widgets	500	1.5	$750
12/21/01	Sam's supply store	Bolts	150	2.75	$412.50
12/27/01	New Hardware	Rivets	200	1.25	$250.00
				Total	$1412.50

At the end of each month, the sales would be added up, and entered into the **General Journal** (discussed below). The source documents such as the invoices that originated the sales and any other paperwork related to the sale would be filed appropriately under each customer's name. Normally the sales shown in this journal would have been made on account and therefore you would expect to see a corresponding entry to the accounts receivable account.

The Purchase or Cash Disbursement Journal (CDJ)

The Purchase Journal is very similar to the sales journal except it records the purchases made by the company either on account or for cash. A large company may have a purchases journal and a separate cash disbursement journal. A smaller company that does not record a large volume of disbursements, on a monthly basis may combine the two journals into one. The cash disbursement journal will normally record all purchases of the company as well as all other disbursements such as the purchase of office supplies (pens, paper, tape etc...). Other expenses may include the payment of rent on the building or payment of utilities such as light, water, gas etc.

A purchase journal will record mostly purchases made from suppliers on account. However it usually carries another column called a "miscellaneous or sundry" column, which would record the items that we mentioned above that do not relate to the main purchase of supplies from vendors. Below is an example of a cash disbursement journal.

48

XYZ Company

Cash Disbursement Journal

Page 2

Date	Vendor	Description	Qty.	Unit $	Sundry	Total $
5/12/01	Jim's Hardware	Lumber	16	$5		$80
5/21/01	ABC Supplies	Nails	250	$0.12		30
5/28/01	Real Estate 1 Co.	Rent			$850	
6/12/01	Culligan H20	Water	5	$12	$60	
		Total			$910	$110

At the end of the accounting period, the amounts would be added up and recorded in the **General Journal (GJ)**. The last column would go under "purchases" and the individual sundry entries would be entered on an item-by-item basis in the same journal.

XYZ Company

General Journal

Page 1

Date	Description	Posting Ref.	Debit	Credit
5/31/01	Purchases	CDJ-2	$110.00	
5/31/01	Accounts payable			$110.00
	To record May 01 purchases on account.			
5/31/01	Rent expense	CDJ-2	$850.00	
5/31/01	Cash			$850.00
	To record rent payment for May 01.			
6/30/01	Water expense	CDJ-2	$60.00	
6/30/01	Cash			$60.00
	To record water expense for the month			
12/31/01	Accounts receivable		$1412.50	
12/31/01	Sales	SJ-3		$1412.50
	To record sales for the month of December			

The entries from the Sales Journal and the Cash Disbursement journal have been posted (recorded) to the General Journal to show how these transactions would flow through the journals. To journalize a transaction, you simply fill in the date, a brief description of the transaction; for example "to record sales for the month of December" You would then enter your amounts in the debit and credit column accordingly always checking your math to make sure that you are in balance.

The "Posting Ref." column serves to identify the source of the entries in the general journal. CDJ-2 means that this entry was taken from the Cash Disbursement Journal, page 2. SJ-3 means that the entry was taken from the Sales Journal on page 3. This way one can always go back to verify the information.

Journal entries

The entries that we have been looking at are called <u>Journal Entries.</u> They are normally recorded in the general journal. You should always keep in mind the idea of the double entry system that we discussed earlier, because every entry that is recorded in the general journal carries the same attribute; that is two or more accounts will be affected by each transaction. The following is an example of a transaction that would affect more than two accounts: XYZ Company sells 2000 widgets to ABC Company at $1.5 each. ABC decides to pay 20% on the purchase and tells XYZ that it will pay the balance in 30 days. In your mind you can begin to put together the journal entry as you visualize what is happening. A sale (revenue account) is created, Cash is received (increase) and a receivable asset is also created (increase). The entry to record this transaction is as follows:

Cash (increase—debit) (2000 x $1.5 x 20%).............................$600
Accounts receivable (increase—debit) (2000 x $1.5 x 80%) .$2,400
Sales (increase—credit) (2000 x $1.5)...................................$3,000
To record sales to ABC company with 20% down and 80% on account.

Notice that the sum of the cash amount and accounts receivable equal the total sales of $3,000. This is important because this assures us that our accounting equation of A = L + OE is in balance. Every journal entry that is journalized (this is an accounting term that means to record journal entries) in the General Journal must balance. If it doesn't, then your equation will be off balance and you will not be able to prepare the financial statements for the company. So make sure that as you journalize your entries they always balance. It is a time consuming thing to have to go back through the journals to find errors you may have made with entries that are off balance.

The General Ledger (GL)

After you have made all of your journal entries for the month or the year, depending on the period for which you are preparing the financial statements, the next step is to post (transfer) all of your entries from the general journal to the General Ledger. The GL is the main book of the company. It holds all of the accounts of the company with their respective balances at any given time. Assuming we were to post from the above GJ to the sample accounts below from the GL, it would look something like the following:

XYZ COMPANY

GENERAL LEDGER

Cash

Date	Description	Post Ref.	Debit	Credit
6/30/01	Cash activities from 5/31 to 12/31/01	GJ-1		$910

Accounts Receivable

Date	Description	Post Ref.	Debit	Credit
7/31/01	AR entries from 5/31 to 12/31/01	GJ-1	$1,412.50	

Rent Expense

Date	Description	Post Ref.	Debit	Credit
7/31/01	Rent exp. activities, 5/31 to 12/31/01	GJ-1	$850	

Notice that each account is separate. When you post from the GJ to the individual accounts in the GL, You will post by account. In other words you will add up ALL entries related to "CASH" in the GJ and post the total to the cash account in the GL. So if you had 10 entries affecting cash, you add all the entries and post the total as a one-line item to the cash account in the GL.

The GL is pretty straightforward. The date is the date when you are making the entry. The description is short and describes the entry you are making. The "post ref." is the same idea as the GJ. It shows the journal you are posting from and the page number.

Subsidiary Ledgers

Subsidiary ledgers are mini ledgers that hold the details of a larger account. Certain accounts that appear on the financial statements will be the sum of many smaller accounts. Accounts receivable is one example of an account that also has its own subsidiary ledger called the accounts receivable subsidiary ledger. The following represents the accounts receivable subsidiary ledger for XYZ Company as of 12/31/01.

XYZ Company
A/R Subsidiary Ledger
As of December 31, 2001

ABC Supplies   **Page 1**

Date	Description	Debit	Credit	Balance
2/15/01	Sales on account	$2,570		$2,570
2/30/01	Payment		1,000	1,570
3/10/01	Payment		570	1,000

Jim's Hardware   **Page 2**

Date	Description	Debit	Credit	Balance
3/15/01	Sales on account	$22,570		$22,570
3/28/01	Payment		8,500	14,070
4/10/01	Payment		4,500	9,570

AAA Lumber — Page 3

Date	Description	Debit	Credit	Balance
5/15/01	Sales on account	$7,200		$7,200
5/30/01	Sales on account	5,375		12,575
4/10/01	Payment		7,945	4,630

Each vendor would most likely occupy at least one page in the whole ledger. Periodically, the individual accounts are added and compared to the main receivable account in the general ledger. Any discrepancies are investigated and adjusted. Accounts payable also holds a subsidiary ledger that would show the details of the activities with individual vendors. The format is very much the same as with all other subsidiary ledgers. Companies will find it necessary to keep these ledgers on accounts that have to be broken down to individual components. Other accounts with sub-ledgers would include inventory, marketable securities, fixed assets etc.

Dantes Joseph Jr.

CHAPTER 4 EXERCISE

1. Which of the following does not represent a source document for recording purpo

    ○   **A** Invoice

    ○   **B** Sales receipt

    ○   **C** General journal

    ○   **D** Purchase order

2. A vendor invoice that has terms of "2% 10 net 30" means that if the invoice i
paid within 30 days you lose the discount.

    ○   **True**

    ○   **False**

3. In which of the following journals or ledgers will you not see debits & cr
columns?

    ○   **A** General journal

    ○   **B** General ledger

    ○   **C** Sales journal

    ○   **D** Subsidiary ledger

4. The general journal will show all of the accounts of a company with their respe
balances at a given time.

    ○   **True**

    ○   **False**

5. A company purchased merchandise totaling $25,000 in the month of December 2
50% of the invoice amount was paid on delivery and the balance will be paid on Januar
2002. Show the journal entry (debit/credit format) required at the time of the purchase.

54

6. A ledger that holds the detail activities of the main account in the general ledger is called a...

[   ]

7. Entries are usually posted to the general ledger on a daily basis.

○ **True**

○ **False**

8. If an accountant wanted to see the total balance in the inventory account as of 12/31/01, he would consult the following ledger / journal.

○ A Subsidiary ledger

○ B General ledger

○ C General journal

○ D Sales journal

9. An accounting term that means to transfer information from the general journal to the general ledger is called...

[   ]

10. The "posting reference" column in the general journal shows where the journal entries are being posted to.

○ **True**

○ **False**

Answer Key:
Chapter 4 exercise

Answer
1 - C
2 - FALSE
3 - C
4 - FALSE
5 - Purchases...$25,000 Accounts Payable..$12,500 Cash..$12,500 To record purchases; half on account and paid cash for half of merchandise.
6 - subsidiary ledger
7 - FALSE
8 - B
9 - Posting
10 - FALSE

Chapter 5

Preparing A Trial Balance & Adjusting Entries

As was mentioned in the beginning, the ultimate goal of accounting is to prepare financial statements. Once we gather, analyze and evaluate the source data, we then post the information to our journals: Sales Journal (sometimes called Cash Receipts Journal), Cash Disbursements Journal, General Journal and finally the General Ledger. I also made the point that we should always make sure that our debits equal our credits when making the journal entries. Here is where you will see the importance of having the accounts in balance.

The Trial Balance (T/B)

The Trial Balance is a summary of all the accounts from the General Ledger arranged in a debit and credit format. This is where the accountant proofs the individual accounts and makes sure they are in balance before proceeding to the adjusting entries and preparing the financial statements. The T/B can also be turned into a worksheet that will make it easier to prepare the financial statements. The T/B is always shown <u>as of</u> a particular date. Consider the following T/B for XYZ Company.

Dantes Joseph Jr.

XYZ Company
Unadjusted Trial Balance
As of December 31, 2001

Accounts	Debit	Credit
Cash	**500**	
Example Bank	10,500	
Accounts Receivable	15,200	
Allowance for doubtful accounts		700
Marketable securities	1,200	
Office Supplies	500	
Inventory	22,150	
Goodwill	3,200	
Patents	1,000	
Fixed Assets	18,000	
Accumulated Depreciation—fixed assets		3,500
Accounts Payable		8,350
Unearned Income		500
Short-term notes payable		1,500
Long-term Debt		3,000
Owner's Equity		32,805
Owner withdrawals	1,000	
Sales		43,450
Returns and allowances on sales	2,200	
Purchases	12,000	
Purchases Returns and allowances		1,000
Purchase Discounts		50
Freight In	125	
Cost of goods sold		
Rent expense	1,500	
Supplies	350	
Depreciation	3,500	
Bad debt expense	700	
Utilities	220	
Insurance	350	

	Simple Accounting	
Repairs and maintenance	500	
Cleaning	98	
Water	50	
Miscellaneous	12	
Total	**94,855**	**94,855**

Dantes Joseph Jr.

Notice that the T/B is in balance. This is a good sign. All the journal entries were done correctly for this company.

Adjusting Entries

In the example to follow you will notice that once the trial balance is in balance, our next step is to make sure that all <u>adjusting entries</u> come into play. The adjusting entries that are posted are the following:

a- Upon a physical count of the office supplies at the end of the year, $350 worth of supplies was found. Therefore we need to record the expense of $150 to reduce the asset to its proper balance.

b- After analyzing the fixed asset account, we came up with an additional $500 of depreciation. At the end of the year, before we prepare the financial statements, we need to bring all expenses and revenue accounts up to date.

c- Finally after a physical inventory count, we find that $9,700 is still on hand. Working out our Cost of goods sold formula, our journal entry is based on the following:

Beginning Inventory		$22,150
Add: Purchases	$12,000	
Add: Freight In	125	
Less: purchase returns	-1,000	
Discounts	-50	11,075
Total available for sale		33,225
Less: Ending inventory		-9,700
Cost of goods sold		$23,525

The following worksheet shows the above entries posted in the adjustments column and referenced by the letters a, b and c. These entries would also be recorded in the general journal as follows:

a - Supplies expense..$150
    Office supplies $150

60

b - Depreciation expense $500
    Accumulated depreciation $500
c - Cost of goods sold $23,525
    Inventory (ending) 9,700
    Purchase returns & allowances 1,000
    Purchase discounts...50
    Freight In 125
    Purchases 12,000
    Inventory (beginning) 22,150
To record adjusting entries at 12/31/2001.

The cost of goods sold entry will zero out the accounts that make up that cost in a periodic inventory system and adjust the opening inventory account. Thus on the Income Statement, the Cost of Goods Sold will be matched directly against Net Sales and the inventory account will reflect the proper balance that was found during the physical count.

Dantes Joseph Jr.

Accounts	Trial Balance Debit	Trial Balance Credit	Adjustments Debit	Adjustments Credit	Adjusted T/A Debit	Adjusted T/A Credit
Cash	500				500	
Example Bank	10,500				10,500	
Accounts Receivable	15,200				15,200	
Allowance for doubtful accounts		700				700
Marketable securities	1,200				1,200	
Office Supplies	500			a-150	350	
Inventory	22,150		c-9,700	c-22,150	9,700	
Goodwill	3,200				3,200	
Patents	1,000				1,000	
Fixed Assets	18,000				18,000	
Accumulated Depreciation—fixed assets		3,500		b-500		4,000
Accounts Payable		8,350				8,350
Unearned Income		500				500
Short-term notes payable		1,500				1,500
Long-term Debt		3,000				3,000
Owner's Equity		32,805				32,805
Owner withdrawals	1,000				1,000	

Sales		43,450				43,450
Returns and allowances on sales	2,200				2,200	
Purchases	12,000			c-12,000		
Purchases Returns and allowances		1,000	c-1,000			
Purchase Discounts		50	c-50			
Freight In	125			c-125		
Cost of goods sold			c-23,525		23,525	
Rent expense	1,500				1,500	
Supplies	350		a-150		500	
Depreciation	3,500		b-500		4,000	
Bad debt expense	700				700	
Utilities	220				220	
Insurance	350				350	
Repairs and maintenance	500				500	
Cleaning	98				98	
Water	50				50	
Miscellaneous	12				12	
Total	94,855	94,855	34,925	34,925	94,305	94,305

Dantes Joseph Jr.

I hope that you have begun to see the whole logic of accounting. The math that we have done so far is very basic. That's why I said in the beginning that one does not have to be a math genius to do well in accounting. The main thing is to be organized, patient and have a willingness to face the challenge of balancing out your accounts.

CHAPTER 5 EXERCISE

1. Describe what the Trial Balance (T/B) is. What is the importance of having its debits equaling credits?

2. What is the difference between an adjusted and an unadjusted trial balance?

3. XYZ Company is getting ready to prepare its financial statements at 12/31/01. The following facts relate to the company at year-end: 1- A bank statement received shows interest earned on a certificate of deposit (CD) of $125. 2- The accountant calculates depreciation on the straight-line method on Furniture & Equipment to be $2,000. 3- The company recorded $1,200 rent paid on 6/30/01 as rent expense. Half of it has been used through 12/31/01. Record (debit/credit format) the adjusting entries required.

4. The "allowance for bad debts" account is shown on the trial balance with a credit balance.

    ◯   **True**

    ◯   **False**

5. The following is not an account used in calculating "cost of goods sold."

    ◯   **A** Purchase discounts

    ◯   **B** Ending inventory

    ◯   **C** Beginning inventory

    ◯   **D** Sales returns & allowances

Dantes Joseph Jr.

Answer key:
Chapter 5 exercise

Answer

1—The Trial Balance is a summary of ALL the accounts of the General Ledger, in debit/credit format, with their respective balances as of a particular date.

It's important to have it in balance because of the "double entry" system. It's a way of proving that all journal entries were properly recorded and debits equaled credits.

2—An unadjusted Trial Balance shows the accounts from the GL before any adjustments are made.

An adjusted Trial Balance shows the same accounts after adjustments like depreciation, supplies etc. are made in preparation for the formal Financial Statements.

3 - Bank or Cash $125
Interest income.. $125
To record $125 interest earned on CD.
Depreciation expense..$2000
Accumulated depreciation $2000
To record depreciation expense on Furniture & Fixtures at year-end.
Advance or prepaid rent...$600
Rent expense $600
To recognize advance rent at year-end and adjust the related rent expense.

4 - TRUE

5 - D

Chapter 6

Financial Statements

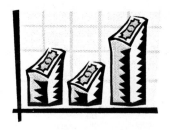

We have come to the moment of truth. The ultimate objective of accounting: to prepare a set of financial statements that will be used by the general public. Accounting is an <u>art</u> and not an exact science. The financials are not designed to be 100% accurate. To use the language of auditors when they audit the numbers, the financial statements should represent "fairly the financial position and results of operation" of a company. The basic financial statements are the Income Statement (sometimes called the Statement of Operations), the Balance Sheet and the Statement of Equity. There is another statement called the Statement of Cash Flow, which we will not cover in this book because it's a little more advance. We will cover the basic, more common, three statements.

The Income Statement

This statement shows the results of operation of a company for a particular period. Normally it covers an entire year. However, it can be prepared quarterly or even monthly depending on the needs of management.

Let's look again at the worksheet that has the adjusted T/B and extend that a little more to give us the basis for our financial statements.

Dantes Joseph Jr.

Accounts	Adjusted T/B Debit	Adjusted T/B Credit	Income Statement Debit	Income Statement Credit	Balance Sheet Debit	Balance Sheet Credit	Owner's Equity Debit	Owner's Equity Credit
Cash	500				500			
Example Bank	10,500				10,500			
Accounts Receivable	15,200				15,200			
Allowance for doubtful accounts		700				700		
Marketable securities	1,200				1,200			
Office Supplies	350				350			
Inventory	9,700				9,700			
Goodwill	3,200				3,200			
Patents	1,000				1,000			
Fixed Assets	18,000				18,000			
Accumulated Depreciation—FA		4,000				4,000		
Accounts Payable		8,350				8,350		
Unearned Income		500				500		
Short-term notes payable		1,500				1,500		
Long-term Debt		3,000				3,000		
Owner's Equity		32,805						32,805
Owner's Drawings	1,000						1,000	
Sales		43,450		43,450				
Returns and allowances on sales	2,200		2,200					
Purchases								
Purchases Returns and allowances								
Purchase Discounts								
Freight In								
Cost of goods sold	23,525		23,525					
Rent expense	1,500		1,500					

Supplies	500				**32,805**
Depreciation	4,000				9,795
Bad debt expense	700				
Utilities	220				
Insurance	350				
Repairs and maintenance	500				
Cleaning	98				
Water	50			1,000	
Miscellaneous	12			41,600	
Total	**33,655**	**43,450**	**59,650**	**18,050**	**1,000**
Net Income for the period	9,795	43,450	59,650	41,600	43,600

OK so we start out with the adjusted T/B and extend our numbers to the income statement column. By adding the revenues and expenses, we find that the company had income of $9,795 because revenues exceeded the expenses. The income gets transferred over to the owner's equity statement because that is additional equity that is credited to the owner of the company. Finally the difference in the balance sheet account ($41,600) is also carried over to the equity statement. The bottom numbers represent balancing figures to prove our entire worksheet.

Another thing I should point out is that the owner's equity is sometimes reduced by personal drawings that he or she makes from the business. In this case the owner withdrew $1,000. This is reflected in the account in the proper column. The drawing account has a normal debit balance.

Now that our worksheet is in balance, it is time to prepare our formal financial statements. This is easy to do because the numbers are already there within the right statement. We always want to start with the income statement in order to determine the net income or loss, which will be carried over to the balance sheet and equity statements.

XYZ Company
Income Statement
For the year ended December 31, 2001

Gross Sales		**$43,450**
Less: Returns and allowances on sales		2,200
Net Sales		**41,250**
Less: Cost of goods sold:		23,525
Gross Profit		**17,725**
Operational Expenses		
Rent	1,500	
Supplies	500	
Depreciation	4,000	
Bad debt expense	700	
Utilities	220	
Insurance	350	
Repairs and maintenance	500	
Cleaning	98	
Water	50	
Miscellaneous	12	7,930
Net Income		**$9,795**

Cost of goods sold is matched right against the net sales because of the matching principle concept. The cost of selling the merchandise is placed right after the sales to calculate the Gross Profit (GP). Gross profit; because you still have to take into account the expenses that are "operational" in nature. They do not directly relate to the selling of merchandise. These are costs of doing business and necessary for the continuing operation of the company.

The sales returns represent items that were sold and later returned for one reason or another. These have to be shown separately and are deducted from sales. This allows management to know exactly the types and quantity or merchandise being returned so that action can be taken to resolve any problem causing the returns.

Dantes Joseph Jr.

The Balance Sheet (BS)

The balance sheet is a statement of the financial position of a company **as of** a particular date. It shows the company's assets, liabilities and equity. Again, this is where you prove the accounting equation because assets have to equal liabilities plus owner's equity. Consider the worksheet in the previous example and see the balance sheet below.

XYZ Company
Balance Sheet
As of December 31, 2001

Current Assets		Current Liabilities	
Cash	$500	Accounts Payable	$8,350
Equitable Bank	10,500	Unearned Income	500
Accounts Receivable		Short-term notes payable	1,500
(Net of $700 of allowances)	14,500		
Marketable securities	1,200	*Non-current liabilities*	
Office Supplies	350	Long-term Debt	3,000
Inventory	9,700	*Total Liabilities*	13,350
Non-current Assets		*Owner's Equity*	
Intangibles		Equity Account	42,600
Goodwill	3,200	Less: Owner's Drawings	1,000
Patents	1,000		
		Total Equity	41,600
Fixed Assets			
Machinery & Equipment			
(Net of $4000 of Accum. Dep.)	14,000		
Total Assets	**$54,950**	*Total Liabilities & OE*	**$54,950**

Notice that the Total equity of $41,600 is made up of the following numbers: Beginning Equity plus the net income minus the

72

owner withdrawals ($32,805 + 9,795—1,000). This format will also serve as the basis of the next statement: the owner's equity statement. Even though all the elements of this statement are already included in the balance sheet, a separate equity statement and disclosure is required to show the activities in the owner's equity account.

The Statement of Owner's Equity

Like the income statement, this statement shows the activity in the equity account for a period of time. In this particular case it is for the whole fiscal year of December 2001.

XYZ Company
Statement of Owner's Equity
For the year ended December 31, 2001

Equity Balance on January 1, 2001	**$32,805**
Add: Income for the year	9,795
Total accumulated equity	**42,600**
Less: Owner's cash withdrawal	1,000
Equity Balance on December 31, 2001	**41,600**

Footnote Disclosure of Accounting Policies

Footnote disclosure is usually required to explain accounting policies used by the company as well as certain unusual items on the financial statements; especially for statements that are being used by the investing public.

Accounting policies include principles and methods used in the presentation of financial statements, including:

- A selection from generally accepted accounting principles
- Unique practices to the industry
- Unusual applications of GAAP.

Dantes Joseph Jr.

The first footnote or section preceding the notes to the financial statements should be a description of the accounting policies followed by the company. They include some the following:

- Depreciation method used
- Amortization period for goodwill
- Inventory pricing method

Although the Financial Accounting Standards Board (FASB) has a variety of regulations on disclosure, the bottom line is to provide accurate information regarding various aspects of the financials. Some types of financial statements do not need a description of the accounting policies followed, such as un-audited quarterly statements where there's been no policy changes from one period to the next and statements that are purely for internal purposes.

Closing Entries

Once the fiscal period comes to an end and the financials have been prepared, you will need to bring all your income and expense accounts to "0" in order to start accumulating data for the next accounting period. To do this, all revenue accounts like sales, other income, commissions etc... need to be debited to bring them to "0". Your expenses will have to be credited to zero them out as well. The difference (income or loss) is carried over to an account called "Income Summary".

You can use the "adjusted trial balance" to pick up the income and expense accounts that you will close. Consider the following closing entries for the above example:

	Debit	Credit
Sales	43,450	
Returns and allowances on sales		2,200
Purchases		12,000
Purchases Returns and allowances	1,000	
Purchase Discounts	50	
Freight In		125
Cost of goods sold		12,450
Rent expense		1,500
Supplies		500
Depreciation		4,000

74

Bad debt expense	700
Utilities	220
Insurance	350
Repairs and maintenance	500
Cleaning	98
Water	50
Miscellaneous	12
Income Summary	9,795

To close Income and Expense accounts for the fiscal year ended 12/31/01.

Some may close the revenue and expense accounts separately; that is to debit sales and credit the income summary and then debit the income summary and credit the expense accounts. I've combined them into ONE entry. The net effect is the same. I've simplified the process by eliminating an extra step. Notice that the net income of $9,795 is credited to Income Summary. All the closing entry does is zero out those accounts in order to prepare them for the next accounting period. You will have to journalize this entry in the general journal and post it to the general ledger just like any other entry. This entry again, should have debits and credits in balance.

Closing the income summary and drawing accounts

The next thing you want to do is to bring the capital account of the owner up to date. This is done by closing both the income summary and the drawing accounts to the owner's capital account. If this were a partnership, each individual capital account would have to be adjusted as well. The following are the entries you would need to adjust the capital account in the above example:

Income Summary (debit—decrease) $9,795
Owner's Equity (credit—increase) $9,795
To close income summary account to the owner's capital at 12/31/01

Owner's Equity (debit—decrease) $1,000
Owner's Drawing (credit—decrease) $1,000
To close owner's drawing account to the owner's equity at 12/31/01

Dantes Joseph Jr.

Post-Closing Trial Balance

After preparing the financials and making the closing entries, you will want to proof your accounts to make sure that you are still in balance. To do this you simply prepare another trial balance called the "post-closing trial balance." This is the same trial balance only without the revenues and expenses because they have been reduced to zero. Once all the closing entries are posted and you verify that the general ledger is in balance, our post-closing trial would look like the following:

XYZ Company
Post-closing Trial Balance
As of December 31, 2001

Accounts	Debit	Credit
Cash	500	
Equitable Bank	10,500	
Accounts Receivable	15,200	
Allowance for doubtful accounts		700
Marketable securities	1,200	
Office Supplies	350	
Inventory	9,700	
Goodwill	3,200	
Patents	1,000	
Fixed Assets	18,000	
Accumulated Depreciation—FA		4,000
Accounts Payable		8,350
Unearned Income		500
Short-term notes payable		1,500
Long-term Debt		3,000
Owner's Equity		41,600
Total	**59,650**	**59,650**

An interesting thing to note here is that the Owner's Equity account of $41,600 ends up being the same as in the "Statement of Owner's Equity"; not surprising of course. We also have the proof that our post-closing trial balance is in perfect balance. You are now ready to start accumulating new revenue, expense and drawing information for the next accounting cycle.

CHAPTER 6 EXERCISE

1. Which of the following is not a basic financial statement?

○ **A** Balance sheet

○ **B** Statement of OE

○ **C** Statement of cash flow

○ **D** Income statement

2. The income statement shows a company's results of operation as of a particular date.

○ **True**

○ **False**

3. Excess revenue over expenses on the income statement is carried over into which statement...

> [   ]

4. The net effect of the Owner's Equity statement is carried over into which of these statements?

○ **A** Income statement

○ **B** Statement of equity

○ **C** Balance sheet

○ **D** Statement of cash flow

5. Information in the financial statements that describes a company's accounting policies and other significant factors affecting the financials are called...

> [   ]

Dantes Joseph Jr.

Answer Key:
Chapter 6 exercise

Answer
1 - C
2 - FALSE
3 - Owner's Equity statement
4 - C
5—Footnote disclosures

Chapter 7

Ratio Analysis

Once the financial statements are prepared we can obviously see the results of operation and the financial position of a company. However there are some decision-making tools that are not readily seen unless the financials are analyzed through ratios. Ratios tell us certain trends that form in a company's ability to manage its debts, collect its outstanding receivables and sell inventory items on hand.

Financial ratio analysis is the calculation and comparison of ratios, which are derived from the information in a company's financial statements. The level and historical trends of these ratios can be used to make inferences about a company's financial condition, its operations and attractiveness as an investment. Here are some of the more common ratios used in the field:

Balance Sheet Ratio Analysis

Important Balance Sheet Ratios measure liquidity and solvency (a business's ability to pay its bills as they come due) and leverage (the extent to which the business is dependent on creditors' funding). They include the following:

Liquidity Ratios
These ratios indicate the ease of turning assets into cash. They include the Current Ratio, Quick Ratio, and Working Capital.

Current Ratios. The Current Ratio is one of the best-known measures of financial strength. It is figured as follows:

$$\text{Current Ratio} = \frac{\text{Total Current Assets}}{\text{Total Current Liabilities}}$$

The main question this ratio addresses is: "Does the company have enough current assets to meet the payment schedule of its current debts." A generally acceptable ratio is 2 to 1. But whether or not a specific ratio is satisfactory depends on the nature of the business and the characteristics of its current assets and liabilities. The minimum acceptable current ratio is obviously 1:1, but that relationship is usually playing it too close.

Quick Ratios. The Quick Ratio is sometimes called the "acid-test" ratio and is one of the best measures of liquidity. It is figured as follows:

$$\text{Quick Ratio} = \frac{\text{Cash} + \text{Government Securities} + \text{Receivables}}{\text{Total Current Liabilities}}$$

The Quick Ratio is a much more exact measure than the Current Ratio. By excluding inventories, it concentrates on the really liquid assets, with value that is fairly certain. It helps answer the question: "If all sales revenues should disappear, could a company meet its current obligations with the readily convertible `quick' funds on hand?"

An acid test of 1:1 is considered satisfactory unless the majority of your "quick assets" are in accounts receivable, and the pattern of accounts receivable collection lags behind the schedule for paying current liabilities.

Working Capital. Working Capital is really a measure of cash flow than a ratio. The result of this calculation must be a positive number. It is calculated as shown below:

Working Capital = Total Current Assets - Total Current Liabilities

Bankers look at Net Working Capital over time to determine a company's ability to face financial crises. Loans are often tied to minimum working capital requirements. A general observation about these three Liquidity Ratios is that the higher they are the better, especially if you are relying to any significant extent on creditor money to finance assets.

Leverage Ratio

This Debt/Worth or Leverage Ratio indicates the extent to which the business is reliant on debt financing (creditor money versus owner's equity):

$$\text{Debt/Worth Ratio} = \frac{\text{Total Liabilities}}{\text{Net Worth}}$$

Generally, the higher this ratio, the more risky a creditor will perceive its exposure in a company, making it correspondingly harder to obtain credit.

Income Statement Ratio Analysis

The following important State of Income Ratios measure profitability:

Gross Margin Ratio

This ratio is the percentage of sales dollars left after subtracting the cost of goods sold from net sales. It measures the percentage of sales dollars remaining (after obtaining or manufacturing the goods sold) available to pay the overhead expenses of the company.

Comparison of a company's business ratios to those of similar businesses will reveal the relative strengths or weaknesses in a business. The Gross Margin Ratio is calculated as follows:

$$\text{Gross Margin Ratio} = \frac{\text{Gross Profit}}{\text{Net Sales}}$$

Net Profit Margin Ratio

This ratio is the percentage of sales dollars left after subtracting the Cost of Goods sold and all expenses, except income taxes. It provides a good opportunity to compare a company's "return on sales" with the performance of other companies in the industry. It is calculated before income tax because tax rates and tax liabilities vary from company to company for a wide variety of reasons, making comparisons after taxes much more difficult. The Net Profit Margin Ratio is calculated as follows:

$$\text{Net Profit Margin Ratio} = \frac{\text{Net Profit Before Tax}}{\text{Net Sales}}$$

Management Ratios

Other important ratios, often referred to as Management Ratios, are also derived from Balance Sheet and Statement of Income information.

Inventory Turnover Ratio

This ratio reveals how well inventory is being managed. It is important because the more times inventory can be turned in a given operating cycle, the greater the profit. The Inventory Turnover Ratio is calculated as follows:

$$\text{Inventory Turnover Ratio} = \frac{\text{Net Sales}}{\text{Average Inventory at Cost}}$$

Accounts Receivable Turnover Ratio

This ratio indicates how well accounts receivable are being collected. If receivables are not collected reasonably in accordance with their terms, management should rethink its collection policy. If receivables are excessively slow in being converted to cash, liquidity could be severely impaired. The Accounts Receivable Turnover Ratio is calculated as follows:

$$\frac{\text{Net Credit Sales/Year}}{365 \text{ Days/Year}} = \text{Daily Credit Sales}$$

$$\text{Accounts Receivable Turnover (in days)} = \frac{\text{Accounts Receivable}}{\text{Daily Credit Sales}}$$

Return on Assets Ratio

This measures how efficiently profits are being generated from the assets employed in the business when compared with the ratios of firms in a similar business. A low ratio in comparison with industry averages indicates an inefficient use of business assets. The Return on Assets Ratio is calculated as follows:

$$\text{Return on Assets} = \frac{\text{Net Profit Before Tax}}{\text{Total Assets}}$$

These Liquidity, Leverage, Profitability, and Management Ratios allow the business owner to identify trends in a business and to compare its progress with the performance of others through data published by various sources. The owner may thus determine the business's relative strengths and weaknesses.

Dantes Joseph Jr.

CHAPTER 7 EXERCISE

1. Which of the following is not a good reason to prepare financial ratios in analyzing financial statements?

   ○   **A** Liquidity

   ○   **B** Leverage

   ○   **C** Assets

   ○   **D** Profitability

2. Another name for "quick ratios" is the "acid-test ratio".

   ○   **True**

   ○   **False**

3. What is the formula used to calculate "working capital"?

4. Ratios normally allow businesses to identify trends and compare their progress with the performance of other businesses in the industry.

   ○   **True**

   ○   **False**

5. What is the main purpose in calculating the "current ratio"?

Answer Key:
Chapter 7 exercise

Answer
1 - C
2 - TRUE
3—Working Capital = Total current assets—total current liabilities
4 - TRUE
5—The main purpose in calculating the current ratio is to see if a company has enough current assets to meet current liability obligations.

Chapter 8

The Accounting Cycle

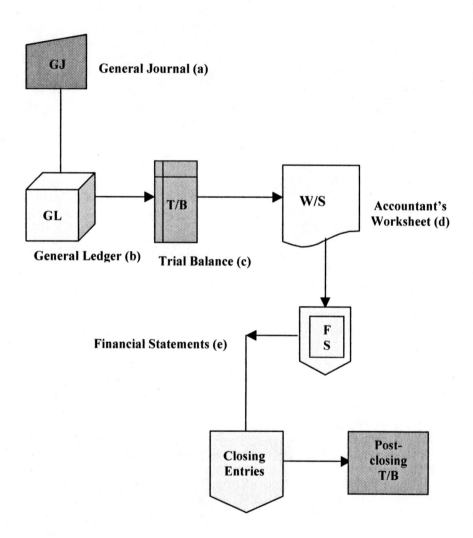

General Journal (a)

GL

General Ledger (b)   Trial Balance (c)

T/B

W/S   Accountant's Worksheet (d)

Financial Statements (e)   F S

Closing Entries   Post-closing T/B

(a) The General Journal is the main journal of the company. This is where all entries are originated. Entries are posted here from the following:

⇒ Sales / Cash receipts journal
⇒ Purchases / Cash Disbursements Journal
⇒ Direct entries by the accountant: like depreciation adjustment, inventory adjustment, adjustments on bad debt expense etc.

(b) The General Ledger is the book that holds all the accounts of the company with their balances. The entries from the general journal are POSTED to the GL. Subsidiary Ledgers are sub ledgers of the GL. They hold detail information on certain accounts from the GL like the following:

⇒ Accounts receivable
⇒ Accounts payable
⇒ Inventory (perpetual)
⇒ Fixed assets etc.

(c) The accounts from the GL are summarized in a debit / credit format into the Trial Balance (unadjusted). The trial balance should balance to prove that the journal entries were posted for the correct amounts in the general journal.

(d) This worksheet is a tool that the accountant uses to facilitate the preparation of the financial statements. It is extended to include the following columns:

⇒ Adjusting entries
⇒ Adjusted trial balance
⇒ Profit & loss column
⇒ Balance sheet column
⇒ A column for the owners equity accounts

Income or loss from the P&L is carried over to the equity column and the difference between the debits and credits column, in the equity section, is carried over to the balance sheet column in order to prove and balance out the entire worksheet.

(e) Once the worksheet is complete and in balance, the formal financial statements are prepared. This is relatively easy because the figures are taken straight from the worksheet. It's simply a matter of putting it in a financial statement format.

Once the financials are prepared, you move on to closing the income and expense accounts and the owner's drawing account to bring them all to a zero balance. They are closed out to the Income Summary account.

Finally you prepare your Post Closing Trial Balance to make sure that your accounts are still in balance and then you are ready to start the next accounting cycle.

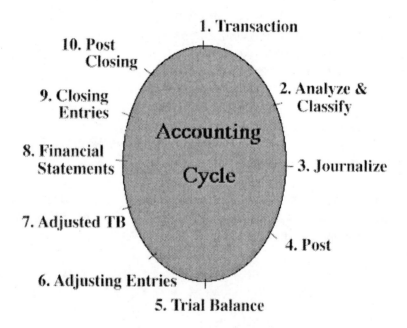

Glossary Of Terms

Account—The device used to record and accumulate individual transactions.

Accounting equation—The equation that establishes the formula for assets, liabilities and equity: $(A = L + OE)$.

Accounts payable—Money that a company owes its vendors.

Accounts receivable—Money owed a company by its customers.

Accounts receivable turnover ratio—A measure of how well accounts receivable are being collected.

Accrual—An accounting method where income and expenses are recorded at the time they incur and not the time in which money changes hand.

Accumulated depreciation—An account used to record and reduce the value of a company's fixed assets. It's known as a contra-asset account.

Adjusting entries—Journal entries that adjust a particular account balance in order to bring that account up to date.

Allowance for bad debt—An account used to reduce the value of A/R by recognizing a % that will not be collected.

American Institute of Certified Public Accountants (AICPA) - A professional organization that provides members with resources, information and leadership that enable them to provide valuable services in the highest professional manner to benefit the public as well as employers and clients.

Amortization—The allocation of the cost of an <u>intangible</u> asset over its useful life.

Assets—What a company owns that has an immediate or future value.

Auditor—One who reviews Financial Statements to determine their fairness in light of Generally Accepted Accounting Principles.

Bad debt expense—Amount that is charged against accounts receivable that the company does not expect to collect.

Balance sheet—A company's basic report showing its financial position as of a particular date.

Cash disbursement journal—See "purchase journal."

Certified Public Accountant (CPA)—See "Auditor."

Closing entries—The journal entry needed at the end of an accounting cycle to bring income and expense accounts to a zero balance. The difference is closed into the Income summary account.

Contra-asset account—An account used to reduce the value of other assets like accounts receivable, fixed assets etc.

Corporation—A business organization recognized by law as a separate entity. Liability is limited only to the assets of the company.

Cost of goods sold—The monetary value of goods sold by a company. It must be matched against "net sales" in order to determine a company's gross profit margin.

Credit—A means of measuring addition and subtraction for different accounts in accounting.

Current Assets—Assets that can be converted into cash within a period of 12 months.

Current Liabilities—Obligations that are due within a 12-month period.

Current ratio—A test that determines whether a company has sufficient current assets to meet its current liabilities.

Debit—A means of measuring addition and subtraction for different accounts in accounting.

Debt/worth ratio—An analysis that determines the extent to which a business is reliant on debt financing.

Depletion—the allocation of the cost of assets of natural resources such as minerals, oil, gas etc.

Deposits in transit—Deposits made by a company that have not yet been processed by the bank.

Depreciation—The allocation of the cost of an asset over its useful life.

Double Declining Balance (DDB)—An accelerated method of depreciation used when the productivity of an asset is expected to be greater in the early years of use.

Double Entry—The law of accounting that says that every transaction must affect at least two accounts.

Estimated useful life—The estimated total years that an asset is expected to last.

Expenses—Costs incurred by a company in the normal course of business.

Financial Accounting Standards Board—A professional organization that establishes and improves standards of financial accounting and reporting for the guidance and education of the general public.

Financial statements—The basic reports of a company that show the results of operation for a specific period and financial position as of a specific date.

First in first out (FIFO)—An inventory valuation method that assigns the cost of the earliest inventory purchases to the cost of goods sold thus resulting in a lower cost of goods sold and a higher ending inventory.

Fixed assets—Long-term assets of a company with useful lives of 12 months or more.

Footnote disclosure—Notes attached to financial statements that disclose a company's accounting policies and certain unusual items related to the financials.

General journal—A journal where all journal entries are recorded in a debit / credit format.

General ledger (GL)—The main accounting book that contains all the accounts of a company with their respective balances.

Generally Accepted Accounting Principles (GAAP)—A set of accounting rules, standards and procedures for recording and reporting financial data to accurately represent an organization's financial condition.

Gross margin ratio—A measure of the percentage of sales dollars available to pay (after obtaining or manufacturing the goods sold) overhead expenses of a company.

Gross profit (margin)—The excess of sales over a company's cost of goods sold.

Income—Monetary benefits received by a company in exchange for products or services.

Income statement—A company's basic report of the results of operations for a specified period.

Income summary—The account to which income or loss is closed out to at the end of an accounting cycle.

Intangible asset—Assets without a physical substance like goodwill, patent etc.

Internal Revenue Service (IRS)—The nation's tax collection agency that provides America's taxpayers with top quality service by helping them understand and meet their tax responsibilities and by applying the tax law with integrity and fairness to all.

Dantes Joseph Jr.

Inventory—Merchandise held for resale.

Inventory turnover ratio—A measure of how well inventory is being managed.

Invoice—An internal document prepared by a company in connection with the sale of merchandise or services.

Journal entries—Accounting entries made in the general journal in debit / credit format.

Journalizing—the process of recording journal entries.

Last in first out (LIFO)—An inventory valuation method that assigns the cost of the most recent inventory purchases to the cost of goods sold thus resulting in a higher cost of goods sold and a lower ending inventory.

Liabilities—Obligations that a company has.

Limited liability—A situation where liability is limited to a business organization like a corporation. Owners of a company are protected from personal lawsuits.

Lower of cost or market (LCM)—The value at which inventory and marketable securities should be recorded.

Marketable securities—A company's investment in temporary stock, bonds, mutual funds etc.

Matching Principle Concept—The accounting rule that says that expenses must be matched to its related revenue within the same accounting period.

Merchandising—A business organization that buys merchandise to sell for a profit.

Net profit margin ratio—A measure of a company's return on sales with the performance of other companies in the industry.

Non-current Assets—Assets with a lifespan of 12 months or more.

Non-current Liabilities—Obligations that have maturity dates of 12 months or more.

Outstanding checks—checks written by a company that have not yet cleared the bank.

Owner's Equity—The difference between assets and liabilities.

Partnership—A business organization where two or more people invest their individual skills and labor to form a company. The owners have unlimited liability.

Periodic Inventory—A method where ending inventory is calculated by taking a physical count at the end of an accounting period. When this is done, cost of goods sold is also calculated to determine a company's gross profit margin.

Perpetual Inventory System—A method of keeping track of the value of inventory on hand. A journal entry is made to this account every time inventory is purchased or sold.

Petty Cash—A certain amount of cash kept on hand by a company for miscellaneous disbursements.

Post—The process of transferring all journal entries to the company's main general ledger.

Post closing trial balance—The trial balance that is prepared after all revenue and expense accounts have been closed to the income summary, and after the income summary and the drawing accounts are closed to the owner's capital account.

Prepaid expenses—current value of future benefits, paid in advance.

Proprietorship—A business organization where one person owns 100% of the business. The owner has unlimited liability.

Purchase journal—A journal where all merchandise purchase of a company as well as other cash disbursements are recorded.

Purchase order (PO)—An internal document generated, by a company, after the purchasing department receives a purchase requisition.

Purchase requisition—An internal document in a company generated by the department desiring to make a purchase.

Quick ratio—A measure of whether or not a company will meet its current obligations with funds on hand if sales should disappear.

Ratio analysis—The process of analyzing financial statements to determine a company's financial strength and weaknesses.

Receiving document—An internal document prepared by a company after receiving merchandise ordered through a purchase order.

Reconciliation—The process of analyzing the transactions that affect two sets of books in order to find the correct balance as of a specific date.

Reconciling items—The transactions that affect two sets of books like outstanding checks, deposits in transit etc.

Return on assets ratio—A measure of how efficiently profits are being generated from the assets employed in a business when compared with the ratios of company's in a similar business.

Revenue—See "Income".

Sales journal—A journal where all the sales of a company are recorded.

Salvage value—The monetary value that an asset is expected to be sold for at the end of its useful life.

Service—A business organization that provides a service for a profit.

Specific Identification Method—An inventory valuation method that assigns exact purchase cost of merchandise to the ending inventory.

Statement of owner's equity—A report used for sole proprietorships that shows the investing activities and details of the capital account of the owner of the company.

Straight-line—The decrease of value of an asset evenly over its useful life.

Subsidiary ledger—A ledger used by a company that contains the detail activities of a master account like accounts receivable, accounts payable, inventory etc.

Sum of the year's digits (SYD)—Another form of accelerated depreciation that assumes that a fixed asset loses a greater portion of its value in the early years of use.

T-accounts—A tool used by accountants, in the form of a "T" to quickly analyze the effects of debits and credits on a particular account.

Timing differences—Reconciling items that do not need to be adjusted. It's only a matter of time before both sets of books reflect those transactions.

Transaction—The legal exchange of items of value such as money paid for services rendered.

Trial balance—A summary of all the accounts from the general ledger arranged in a debit / credit format.

Unearned revenue—Money received in advance and not yet earned. It becomes a liability.

Units of production (UOP)—A method of depreciation that takes into account the actual units that an asset produces over its useful life.

Unlimited liability—To be personally and individually liable for debts or damages in a lawsuit.

Weighted average—An inventory valuation method that assigns the average cost of merchandise purchased to both ending inventory and cost of goods sold.

Working capital—A measure of cash flow that shows just how much liquid funds a company has after subtracting current liabilities from current assets.

Dantes Joseph Jr.

About the Author

Dantes Joseph Jr. is an accountant who graduated with a bachelor's degree from Jersey City State College in May of 1987. He also holds an associate's degree from Rockland County Community college. He worked as an auditor, controller and senior/staff accountant for 14 years for various companies including *Touche Ross*—a former big eight accounting firm. Accounting is his favorite subject. He carried a 4.0 grade point average (GPA) in it through his advance accounting courses in school. He then realized that at the age of 40, it's more rewarding to share his knowledge and expertise with others who are either getting started in the accounting field or are struggling with it. Being conscious of the difficulties that new students to accounting will face, he decided to use his own experience to simplify the fundamental accounting principles that college students will have to face. His main goal is to use the same material that is taught in college and simplify it through examples, shortcuts, spreadsheets and flowcharts so students may understand the material more easily.

Mr. Joseph is also an active real estate investor. He owns a few investments properties. He is also the owner and president of DJ Accounting & Tax Services: a practice that specializes in performing computerized accounting, bookkeeping and tax in Miami Florida.

Website: www.dj3enterprise.com

Printed in the United States
49141LVS00003B/122